# Praise for *Trailblazers*

"As a former CEO of Southwest Airlines, I think *Trailblazers* presents a comprehensive and compelling framework for what it really takes for organizations and leaders to be successful in a multicultural world. *Trailblazers* provides an in depth and well organized look at all the components and requirements of strategic diversity and inclusion, as well as a discerning look at the motivation and leadership skills of twelve highly respected chief diversity officers."

—Howard Putnam
Former CEO Southwest Airlines
Author of *The Winds of Turbulence*

"If someone in leadership does not intellectually understand and fully internalize the business case of a changing workforce, global marketplace and community, they disqualify themselves from leadership. Lenora and Redia go beyond the business case for diversity and inclusion in this book. *Trailblazers* provides compelling evidence and best practices that clearly integrate diversity and inclusion into successful leadership and business success."

—Frank J. McCloskey
Vice President Diversity
Georgia Power

"This book is truly a 'keeper' for business leaders who want their organizations to be on the cutting edge of diversity and inclusion strategies—and most importantly, achieve meaningful results. The authors do a great job of providing compelling insights, practical approaches and wisdom as told through the hands-on experiences of diversity gurus."

—Claudette J. Whiting
President of CJW Consulting and Former head of Diversity
and Inclusion for Microsoft and The DuPont Company

"*Trailblazers* provides an insightful look into the practical strategies implemented by some of the most respected leaders in diversity and inclusion. Their results-producing approaches in top corporations give clear and compelling guidance to all those who are working to leverage diversity's potential and create environments where talent thrives for the good of all."

—Anita Rowe, PhD
Partner, Gardenswartz & Rowe
Co-author, Managing Diversity: A Complete Desk
Reference and Planning Guide, Revised Edition

"This insightful work explores the multicultural dynamic from a meaningful business and social perspective. It guides us all in the right directions for a more productive and meaningful approach to organizational success. As the world becomes a smaller or more tightly knit place, this book highlights how best to use an organization's strongest asset: its people."

—Dr. Nido Qubein
President, High Point University
Chairman, Great Harvest Bread Co.

"*Trailblazers* is an impressive compilation of diversity and inclusion advice from some of the most admired companies in the world. Using real time business examples, *Trailblazers* does an outstanding job of defining diversity and inclusion as a business imperative. Many companies still believe that diversity and inclusion is just a strategy to avoid litigation and protect revenue. For those organizations that are still confused about the business case for leading with a diversity and inclusion mindset, this book sets the record straight and is a book those organization's leaders should read."

—H. Joseph Machicote
VP, Talent Management & HR Services
Lance, Inc.

"*Trailblazers* is an important contribution to the diversity literature. It focuses more on results than on rhetoric, and takes us past diversity training to effective diversity strategies. So many myths are tackled in this book that it is a must-read for diversity practitioners and those they report to. If just one-tenth of the suggestions in this book were implemented, the workplace would be far more inclusive, and, equally importantly, more productive."

—Dr. Julianne Malveaux
President, Bennett College for Women
Economist and regular guest columnist for *USA Today*

"*Trailblazers* presents a comprehensive and compelling framework for what it really takes for organizations and accountable leaders to be successful in a multicultural world. Whether your organization is global or regional, the insightful best practices [that] award winning companies have provided will help you make diversity a competitive advantage."

—Sam Silverstein
Author: *No More Excuses*
Past President of The National Speakers Association

"This book provides an insightful and much needed look into the life stories, motivations, and challenges of leaders in diversity work. It illuminates how they navigated their roles as agents for those traditionally excluded and the business imperatives of the organisations in which they are employed. There are many lessons and practical strategies for all who wish to do diversity work, no matter what part of the world you live in."

—Professor Stella M. Nkomo
University of Pretoria, South Africa
Co-author, *Our Separate Ways:*
*Black and White Women and the Struggle for Professional Identity*

"Like the Chief Diversity Officers who inspired the title, the authors of *Trailblazers* have provided the reader with fresh and innovative practices that will help drive forward any company's diversity/inclusion efforts. By laying out the wisdom of CDO's who have on the ground, in the trenches experience, the book serves as a practical resource for anyone with a commitment to achieving the business success that only a truly inclusive workplace can provide."

—Sondra Thiederman, PhD
Author of *Making Diversity Work:*
*Seven Steps for Defeating Bias in the Workplace*

# TRAIL BLAZERS

## HOW TOP BUSINESS LEADERS ARE ACCELERATING RESULTS THROUGH INCLUSION AND DIVERSITY

## REDIA ANDERSON & LENORA BILLINGS-HARRIS

WILEY

John Wiley & Sons, Inc.

Published by John Wiley & Sons, Inc., Hoboken, New Jersey.
Published simultaneously in Canada.

For general information on our other products and services or for technical support, please contact our Customer Care Department within the United States at (800) 762-2974, outside the United States at (317) 572-3993 or fax (317) 572-4002.

Wiley also publishes its books in a variety of electronic formats. Some content that appears in print may not be available in electronic books. For more information about Wiley products, visit our web site at www.wiley.com.

ISBN 978-0-470-59347-9 (cloth); ISBN 978-0-470-88108-8 (ebk); 978-0-470-88109-5 (ebk); 978-0-470-88110-1 (ebk)

Printed in the United States of America

10 9 8 7 6 5 4 3 2 1

*To all the Trailblazers, known and unknown,*
*who have made the present possible,*
*and the future one of great possibilities.*

# Contents

# Foreword

I entered the workforce after graduating from Harvard Business School in 1980. It was a time when there were not many women in business and almost none in line operating roles or roles with responsibility for managing a bottom line, particularly in my industry, the energy industry.

I remember routinely being asked by colleagues to answer the phone and take messages after normal business hours when the administrative assistants had left for the day, or to make copies, or to take notes in the meetings. I don't recall my male colleagues who were also new hires being asked to do these things. I learned to either pitch in and do it or turn down these "opportunities" with grace, lest I be labeled forever with the dreaded "B" word. Getting the balance right between acquiescence (to fit in and be a team player) and defiance (to establish appropriate boundaries and prevent being discounted) was a carefully honed skill that could mean the difference between derailment and progression.

Workplaces all over the United States have changed dramatically for the better in the last 30 years as it pertains to respect and opportunities for women. Women have risen to the top of companies, sitting in the C suite and on boards. This is even occurring in previously male dominated fields such as energy, mining, and chemicals.

While the progress has been significant for Caucasian women, there is still a long way to go and even a longer way to go for men and women of color. According to the *White House Project Report—Benchmarking Women's Leadership*, women now make up over half of managers and professionals in the U.S. workforce but in 2008 were only 3% of CEOs, 15% of board seats, and 6% of the top paying positions of

Fortune 500 companies. Pay disparities between men and women persist, and a survey of media stories suggests that women in power are largely disliked. Catalyst published a report in 2007 called *The Double-Bind Dilemma for Women in Leadership: Dammed if You Do, Doomed if You Don't*. They conclude that women are perceived as competent or likable but rarely both. If women behave consistently with gender stereotypes they are viewed as less competent, and if they act inconsistently they are considered unfeminine.

The women who have made it to the C suite and on boards are trailblazers and pioneers themselves. If they were lucky, as I was, they may have had the good fortune to work for a company that was also a trailblazer. I like the term because it conjures up the image of a journey. Yes, it has been a journey where progress has been made, but there is much progress yet to be had. I am looking forward to the time when it is not considered news to have a woman CEO or a woman board member.

I am deeply honored to be asked to write the foreword for this book. In my personal journey as a leader trying to achieve diversity objectives that positively impact the bottom line, I have had the benefit of learning many lessons from trailblazers. One lesson that vividly comes to mind was taught by the CEO of Shell Oil Company in the mid-1990s. He and I were having a conversation about workforce representation targets and selecting talent. My position was that leaders should always select the best candidate for the job regardless of gender or ethnicity. He taught me that as long as there are underrepresented groups relative to availability in the talent pool, you should hire qualified candidates and you should set representation targets to ensure you are getting at least your fair share of all the available talent. Otherwise you are not likely to reach representation that meets availability because "best" is largely defined by a selector who has biases they are not even aware they have. It is a powerful concept that I still use and teach to others.

*Trailblazers* will provide important insights to leaders grappling with the challenges of attracting and retaining talent from an increasingly diverse talent pool, in every way. The trailblazers portrayed in this book have already experienced the benefits of learning that creating an environment that is positive for less represented segments of the population, like women and people of color and persons with disabilities, creates a more inclusive environment for everyone, which optimizes the skills and capabilities of the entire organization.

The journey continues . . .

—Lynn Laverty Elsenhans
Chairman, CEO, and President of Sunoco Inc.

# Acknowledgments

I t is only fitting that a book of this nature be developed through collaboration. In the true spirit of inclusion and diversity this book is an outcome not only of the authors' experiences and knowledge but of the many others who provided their wisdom and insights as well. To everyone who made this book possible, we say a heartfelt "thank you."

This book has been in the making for several years. In fact, we can fondly recall the exact diversity conference that Lenora and I attended where this idea was born. During a hallway conversation at a break, both Lenora and I agreed that we should write a book. We were certain that a book of this nature did not exist, and that we had a contribution to make to this field and to this body of knowledge. Over the years and through our individual work we've demonstrated that we are strong believers in our obligation to help others navigate and succeed at being successful leaders. We hold a special affinity in particular for Chief Diversity Officers who lead and drive organizational change. It was on that day that a seed was planted.

Little did we know that it would be several years before we would actually begin to take action on that seminal idea. We believe that like fine wine, some ideas get better with time and that there is a time for everything. This book was born of a sincere desire to share our personal expertise and the considerable body of knowledge residing within the brains of experienced, successful Chief Diversity Officers (CDOs), those individuals whom we call Trailblazers in this book: leaders who don't have the time themselves—after all they do have day jobs—to open up their brains and make their knowledge available to others in a written form such as this book. That's where Lenora and I come in. We appreciate what it takes to successfully engage organizations and people in change management, and implement robust and successful inclusion and diversity efforts that make a difference.

## Redia Acknowledges . . .

My awesome young adult children, Jarred and Taylor Payne, have long been a strong sense of purpose and support for me and the work I do. Both millennials, they have taught me much about connecting, engaging, and being inclusive far beyond what I felt I already knew. Their patience, willingness to eat take-out food, and chip in more around the house without complaining—which is significant—is appreciated more than they know. They've never failed to support me in whatever I do. They are reminders to me of the promise of the future and the beauty of what life today is really all about. My 85-year-old father, Tommie J. Anderson, and my sister, Regina C. Anderson, have been absolute bedrocks of support and encouragement for me as well. For all of this, I am truly grateful to be blessed with such wonderful people who are my family.

I thank my National Speakers Association CPR Mastermind group, who offered encouragement and subtle advice along the way. Many thanks to my virtual assistant, Diane Muniz Chong, whose organizational skills kept me straight and sane on many occasions when the administrative aspects of book writing and publishing could seem daunting.

## Lenora Acknowledges . . .

I am blessed to be surrounded by people who are as excited about this book as I am. To my husband, Charles, I am so grateful for your quiet support, patience, and understanding that allowed me to write freely. I thank Chris Clarke-Epstein and Marilynn Semonick, who are my true writing muses. I thank all of my National Speakers Association colleagues and friends who so willingly shared their points of view and suggestions for various aspects of this book. A special thanks to members and authors Francine Ward, Ron Karr, Sam Silverstein, Philip Van Hooser, and Leslie Charles. Thanks to Dr. Holly Buttner and Dr. Kevin Lowe who invited me to partner with them—our research work together adds validity to the anecdotal evidence gathered for this important work. Thanks also to Robert Tutsky for providing the interior graphics, and Gerald Hedlund for providing editing and formatting.

To my office guru, Cynthia Jones, I could not have done this without you. And be advised, I will be calling on you again.

## We Acknowledge . . .

We wish to thank our John Wiley & Sons partners who helped us every step of the way and were our constant companions throughout this process. Christine Moore, the assistant development editor who read every chapter, and did her best to keep us from being too wordy when more simple and straightforward language would do. Lauren Lynch, our associate editor, who was with us from the beginning and who kept the big picture before us and helped us manage those forever fast-approaching deadlines. We'd like also to thank our senior production editor, Deborah Schindlar, who with her keen eyes and sense of clarity spurred us on to make this book resonate as one of the best cutting-edge books of its kind that we could make it.

Finally, there would be no book without the unselfish participation of the Trailblazers. Each of the Trailblazer CDOs profiled in this book is recognized among our peers for the robust and effective inclusion and diversity work they lead in their respective organizations. As each person learned what Lenora and I were planning to do, we were met with such support that it was truly rewarding and heartwarming. Each graciously agreed to participate and willingly shared their considerable insights and knowledge with the intent of helping other leaders learn and gain greater traction with implementing and sustaining inclusion and diversity in their organizations. We believe that the many people who take the time to read this book will receive the benefit of great insights and knowledge and will have an opportunity to peer through the windows and into the mindsets and efforts of the Trailblazers, leaders and human beings who lead enterprise-wide organizational change. To our Trailblazers, we are forever indebted and we say, "Thank you."

Our journey continues . . .

# Preface

Be honest with us. Could your inclusion and diversity efforts use a little help?

If so, you're not alone. Many books have been written about inclusion and diversity over the years—some of them very good books that focus almost exclusively on the extremely important and complex work itself. There are a lot of components associated with how effective these efforts are; elements that must be leveraged to realize maximum results. However, we believe that one key factor associated with effective inclusion and diversity efforts has been consistently overlooked.

Until now, few—if any—books have specifically explored the significance of the role of the Chief Diversity Officer (CDO) with regard to an organization's ability to optimize talent and performance through inclusion and diversity. These leaders have been the engine of change within many successful organizations. CDOs provide a clear voice of what's needed both now and in the future for business success. They emphasize the importance of recognizing the value, engagement, and utilization of all talent with respect to marketplace advantage.

CDOs are at the helm of driving focus, fueling commitment, and collaborating with other key leaders inside and outside their organizations, as well as addressing the concept of an inclusive and engaged workforce. They see how vital inclusion and diversity are to strengthening the fabric of their organizations through a robust pipeline of talent, while also striving to enhance their marketplace presence. They have a clear vision of the advantages and impact of an inclusive and engaged workforce. They "see around corners" with respect to trends and challenges that will impact their organizations' ability to stay relevant in service of a very diverse workplace and marketplace—both in the United States and abroad.

CDOs demonstrate a great deal of ownership for making progress with the inclusion of all talent a reality. They feel compelled to share their knowledge and experiences. Planting seeds, building organizational champions, developing sponsors, enhancing their organizations' presence in the marketplace, and bridging the gap to the communities they serve all allow the CDOs to extend their reach far beyond what they might otherwise provide. And these actions are just a few of the approaches that effective CDOs utilize when they tell us that "it takes a village" to move the dial and advance inclusion and diversity in their organizations and the overall marketplace. Seeing far into the future (horizontally) and deeply into their own organizations (vertically), they identify gaps, create and/or enhance existing solutions to people processes, and tailor interventions that will help their firms grow more profitable by managing the human capital side of the equation. CDOs amplify the points of connectivity and surface area contact between the organization and its people; and, in so doing, increase the impact that diverse talent has on solutions for their customers. This is the work of the Trailblazers we speak of here.

Very little has been revealed about what makes these Trailblazer CDOs so effective. The people we interviewed for this book are compelled to make a difference. While many of them have held other roles in their organizations—finance, operations, HR, legal—working as a CDO is something to which they are each intensely committed. They feel that it provides a tight alignment between their values and their belief in equity. The energy and passion with which the Trailblazers speak and the examples of challenges they have overcome—some of which we'll discuss later in this book—are testaments to their commitment. They believe that their work provides their organizations with a competitive advantage and makes a difference to their people. Each of the Trailblazers has shared unique and very personal stories regarding why they accepted such a role and why they choose to continue in this capacity. We believe you'll see—just as we did—why fostering an inclusive workplace is more than a simple role assignment for these Trailblazers.

Every one of our Trailblazers has a role classified as a senior leadership position. And yet these positions are often the least understood in terms of their impact and influence upon the organization, except to other members of the senior leadership team. In these positions—

which have no parallel role in the organization—the Trailblazers often stand out and stand alone as catalysts for educating people, igniting change, and maintaining a certain level of constructive tension for achieving inclusion results. One of the Trailblazers likened it to driving a car and trying to change the tires at the same time; in other words, it's no small feat.

The Trailblazers—due to their very nature and personal values—have defined their own roles based on business strategy, acumen, and their own sense of fairness and equality. They meld these attributes with thought leadership, passion, and a strong focus on results to steer entire organizations to states of greater consciousness regarding the importance of inclusion and diversity.

What Trailblazers understand better than most is that inclusion and diversity deliver *results*. They are not merely buzzwords but are real-time factors that influence behavior and can make the difference between a successful organization where there are "scratch marks on the door from where people are trying to get into the company"—as one oil and gas CEO would fondly say when speaking about talent acquisition and retention strategies—and an organization where people simply can't wait to get out. These Trailblazers provide a strong commitment to talent utilization, which makes their efforts toward inclusion and diversity highly relevant to everyone in their businesses. They understand the powerful interaction between leveraging talent, inclusion, and diversity, and positioning their organizations more firmly for sustainable growth and success. Magda Yrizarry—Verizon's Vice President of Workplace Culture, Diversity and Compliance—had the following to say about business relevance: "Whether it's a wireless service, the latest in broadband technology, or the best in entertainment, Verizon depends on the unique talents, perspectives, and experiences of our diverse pool of employees to maintain its premier network and better serve our customers."

We call these CDOs Trailblazers because they fully comprehend inclusion and diversity's competitive advantage in the marketplace; and we believe they're doing a lot of things right. Throughout this book, we'll bring you examples of the significant work that Trailblazers from companies such as Verizon, IBM, Merck, Shell, The Coca-Cola Company, Citi, Dell, Ford, Andrews Kurth, Sodexo, American Airlines, and Pitney Bowes are doing, and the outcomes they are achieving as a result of this work. Together, these 12 Trailblazers have over 160 years of experiences to share. Most are benchmarked by other organizations for their commitment to outstanding long-term results. Several of them have received numerous awards and external recognitions for their accomplishments within their firms. The Trailblazers cited in this book came into their roles from a variety of industries: financial services, telecommunications, pharmaceuticals, technology, oil and gas, consumer products, automotive, and more. It seems quite fitting that, in the field of diversity and inclusion, the range of backgrounds among CDOs would be a testament to the belief that diverse perspectives can yield more effective results.

Successful leaders build and influence strategy that propels change. It is our intent to provide you with an unbiased perspective of what it takes to be a Trailblazer. You'll also learn that, while leadership skills and credibility are vitally important in this role, they are only table stakes for what it takes to successfully leverage inclusion and diversity. We noticed in many of our interviews that these Trailblazers go a step further. They recognize and speak directly to the emotional intelligence within their organizations' cultures and boldly state that the "feel" of an organization—with a successful inclusion and diversity effort—encourages an environment of mutual respect, fairness, and reciprocal trust. They strongly believe that organizations that aggressively address and eliminate barriers—real or perceived—encourage collaborative, trust-based relationships, and are better equipped to fully engage their workforce and deliver greater value to their customers.

Whether you're a CDO who is responsible for driving inclusion and diversity efforts deeper into your organization and want to become more effective, or you aspire to become a CDO—this book is for you. If you're an employee who wants to become more engaged in these efforts but aren't sure how or where to plug in, you'll learn more about how to align with this work and identify where you might more fully engage to become part of the solution. Or perhaps you are a manager who already recognizes the worth of inclusion and diversity to your business; you will learn more about how you can step up your contribution and collaboration to drive greater results. Students who hope to join forwarding-thinking organizations and are wondering what to look for amongst the many companies that claim to have robust and inclusive cultures will find that this book enables you to develop an informed point of view by which to screen your top choices.

Whatever the reason for your interest—and we understand there are many to ponder—you'll find insights to provide you with knowledge and insertion points to more fully engage and hold yourself and others accountable for the outcomes of an inclusive and diverse workplace. In all these circumstances, we believe this book will be a helpful guide for understanding the business drivers for helping organizations galvanize resources and implement strategies and best practices to make a sustainable difference.

The organizations presented in the following pages understand that the term *diversity* is not "code" or camouflage for affirmative action. Said differently: It is insufficient to simply discuss and track how many women, people of color, or other kinds of minorities are represented in an organization. What about other conventional and nonconventional forms of diversity? This antiquated view doesn't do justice to the reality of how inclusion and diversity uniquely support the business strategy.

According to a recent survey by Robert Half Management of top executives from the nation's 1,000 largest companies, 61 percent of companies are doing more global business today than they were five years ago. In today's global economy—where it is more common than not for businesses to operate across borders and multiple countries—diversity represents a host of meanings, depending on the countries in which you operate. Diversity in its broadest and simplest form refers to all the ways in which we are different, seen and unseen; inclusion refers to how we utilize those differences in service of our people, and growth and profitability for our businesses.

The prevailing view of the companies cited within these pages focuses on diversity of thoughts, ideas, and perspectives, particularly as it relates to the development of better solutions for clients and customers. These concepts are woven into the ways that these firms and their leaders engage their employees, in the ways employees engage their coworkers, and in the ways these companies connect with and satisfy their customers every day.

Trailblazers and their companies have made significant progress by approaching diversity and inclusion as a business imperative with bottom-line, quantifiable financial impact. Internally, they have made many human resource practices more overtly inclusive. They have connected these practices to business growth by addressing talent management issues and focusing on hiring, advancement, retention, and development. Externally, they've concentrated on enhancing their brand in the marketplace as an inclusive, inviting, and progressive employer where people want to come and grow their careers. The Trailblazers' goals are to increase the odds of their organizations in winning the war for talent, enhancing a culture of inclusion to retain their top performers, and differentiate their organizations in the marketplace.

The Internet has allowed savvy prospective employees to aggressively research and target companies that overtly announce how vital diversity and inclusion are for their staff and clients. Numerous web sites, such as vault.com, help prospective and current employees alike share information about various firms' culture, challenges, and unique celebrations. Information regarding perceptions of how these companies provide challenging assignments for growth and development, compensation, and rewarding employees (or not) is widely available. In addition, one has only to view their friend's Facebook pages or follow Twitter and other social networking sites to learn more than you might want to know regarding individuals'— "and even their peers"—experiences and impressions of XYZ Company. Want to get another perspective of what your employees think of your organization? Visit some of these sites and social media pages for yourself. Grab a cup of coffee, search under the groups tab—and plan to be engrossed with reading others' personal accounts for some time.

What makes our Trailblazer companies so different? Commitment. They're committed to the long view that inclusive practices help promote a culture of fairness, retain top performers, and encourage the broader minority- and women-owned supplier participation (MWBE) that have robust development programs for all their people. In many cases, it's the proven track record of identifying and providing innovative talent solutions that deliver customer problem resolution well in advance of when they are actually needed. Trailblazers anticipate issues and work to constantly update and apply their understanding of global employees' and customers' unique needs to increase relevancy in the ever-changing marketplace.

This book will help leaders, managers, diversity practitioners, academicians, and others refresh and expand their approach to diversity and inclusion. Trailblazers provide insights that will help readers tap into some of the most effective best practices utilized by top-performing companies and their CDOs. This book may be used as a resource guide to prompt any inclusion and diversity efforts that may have plateaued to gain new momentum, reenergize, and set new objectives. This book can become a resource for effective, practical, proven knowledge of bottom-line impact of strategies and accomplishments.

We recognize that individuals who are asked to lead inclusion and diversity efforts have very few books from which to choose—at least, those that also provide first-person perspectives on how to articulate and implement these strategies from the inside out. Because we bring a set of skills that represent strategist, practitioner, organizational change leader, and training consultant, we have been able to target and collect some of the best insights from the Trailblazers who successfully drive inclusion results in their companies and industries. We believe that this book can help the many managers and employees who want to know more about accelerating their progress and driving results by laying bare some of the essential processes, approaches, challenges, and dilemmas the Trailblazers have encountered—and the solutions they've utilized to overcome them.

Vision, strategy, and metrics—*plus* a passion for driving outcomes—yield progress. One of the most effective means to reducing the huge learning curve associated with less mature inclusion and diversity efforts is to expose successful CDOs and their shared experiences around key learnings that can accelerate progress. This book will provide practical examples of where specifically these Trailblazers have contributed to the body of knowledge regarding successful implementation strategies of inclusion and diversity practices that may be helpful to the reader as well. We'll share Inclusion Insights in most chapters to use as a thumbnail guide to simplify and condense key points from that chapter.

We know that there is—as with any other business strategy—a defined process for implementing inclusion and diversity. To that end, we share a five-step strategic method for embedding and advancing inclusion and diversity. We feel that this will be helpful to any organization, no matter what industry or in what stage of the inclusion process they may be engaged. Following a defined plan of action helps to ensure that key levers are addressed and that the effort is on track to deliver results. Such a guide confirms that key practices are not overlooked and actually become incorporated. It makes certain that the inclusion and diversity process is systemically embedded in existing processes that regularly drive accountability and monitor change management progress.

The companies that are cited in the following pages of this book clearly "get it." They can demonstrate and articulate the ROI of inclusion and diversity and explain exactly how it benefits their organizations on multiple levels. We believe these insights will help the reader to jump-start, rev up, and fine-tune existing diversity and inclusion efforts—so that their organizations can yield greater results.

Finally, it is our desire in writing this book to explore and make transparent the strategies, tactics, and processes required to implement, advance, and sustain an effective inclusion and diversity effort. This book will help organizations better position themselves to reap the benefits that the promise of diversity and the power of inclusion bestow.

# 1

# Meet the Trailblazers

*"Don't bother just to be better than your contemporaries
or predecessors. Try to be better than yourself."*
—William Faulkner

Industry leaders—especially those determined to build a culture of inclusion and diversity within their organizations—are becoming more abundant. You don't have to look far to see the effects of the efforts that so many visionary people have made in industry as well as in society. They are often unsung heroes that step up, face the unknown, and move forth in sometimes the darkest hours, clutching the belief that what they do now will have a lasting impact on others for years, and generations, to come.

These Trailblazers, as we will refer to them in this book, each have a story to go along with their incredible efforts and accomplishments. Each was carefully chosen to exemplify the true spirit of not only diversity and inclusion, but also of holding true to one's own and the organization's values.

As we conducted our interviews, what became apparent was that each person had unique experiences and stories, which shaped their views and behaviors regarding inclusion at a relatively young age. Each individual we've spotlighted has faced many challenges along their journey. Rather than accept what was good enough and handing down the idea of a system that wasn't effective to the next generation, they instead focused on actions to create a better tomorrow for everyone.

All of these incredible people, both men and women, are pioneers in their fields. Many of them have worked for and led diversity and inclusion initiatives in more than one organization, moving forward to continue paving—and trailblazing—the way for others who will ultimately follow. These Trailblazers deserve more than they would accept, and ultimately, this qualifies them as true leaders of our age.

It's important that you get the chance to know each of these individuals from the outset. We want you to understand where they come from, what helped to guide them to their true calling, and what continues to inspire them to this day. Strangers are easily dismissed, but those with whom we become familiar can often inspire and instill hope in others to move toward the dreams and paths they have begun to lay out.

Take a moment to meet these 12 inspiring individuals we interviewed. Meet the 12 Trailblazers who have accomplished incredible objectives and continue to instill the benefits of inclusion and diversity within their organizations.

> *"The most dangerous phrase in the language is, 'We've always done it this way.'"*
> —Rear Admiral Grace M. Hopper, U.S. Navy

## Michael Collins

### Managing Director of Diversity Strategies, American Airlines

 The passion that inspires Michael Collins in the field of diversity and inclusion was sown at an early age. The son of a Baptist minister, Michael came into his faith when he was around 9 or 10. His faith puts forth the basic premise that all people matter, that everyone makes a difference. The color of your skin or where you come from doesn't matter; *everyone* is valuable.

Growing up in an environment of inclusion certainly had its impact on Michael's professional life. The concepts to which a person is introduced and with which he is surrounded can have a lasting impact on the rest of his life. Michael certainly captured that essence and carried it with him through his professional career.

In 1989, Michael Collins started his diversity work with true passion and desire. American Express was beginning to consider the concepts of diversity and inclusion within their business model. The company opened a new operations center in Greensboro, North Carolina, that was facing a much different workforce than any of its others. A large portion of the staff included highly educated African Americans; and the need to retain these employees for the long term meant that American Express would have to provide broader opportunities for advancement. Another issue that faced the company also had to do with maintaining satisfaction among all the employees as well as the community.

Michael Collins was only one of two African American managers at his level or higher at the time, and the company had already noticed his potential. While excelling in a leadership role that included managing two large groups, he developed a quality reputation within the organization. It was at this time that he began to research the idea and concept of diversity and inclusion.

Michael took it upon himself to present some innovative ideas to his leadership team. Due to his ambition and passion, American Express asked Michael to participate in helping them to develop a diversity strategy for the entire company. This allowed Michael to delve even deeper into the value of diversity and see how it impacts not only employee satisfaction and well-being, but productivity as well. The more he learned, the more he knew that this was what he wanted to do with his professional life. Michael has devoted 21 years so far to the field of diversity and inclusion. Today, with American Airlines, Michael has become an integral part of their continued growth and leadership with regard to diversity and inclusion.

As stated in American Airlines' Diversity Statement, "By encouraging and supporting the talents of diverse people, we've created a rich tapestry of engaged, dynamic teams, all committed to our airline. Our focus on diversity and inclusion is felt by our customers, employees, and the communities we serve around the world. We remain steadfast in the important everyday work of bringing people together through diversity and inclusion" (www.aa .com/i18n/aboutUs/diversityInclusion/leadershipSidebar.jsp).

### Company Profile
### American Airlines

GERARD J. ARPEY, CEO

- Second largest airline in the industry.
- Encompasses American, American Eagle, and American Connection.
- Serves 250 cities in over 40 countries.
- Manages over 4,000 flights per day and has a workforce of nearly 80,000 employees.
- A founding member of the Global OneWorld Alliance, which unites the biggest names in the industry to offer more destinations and benefits than any single airline can offer.
- The first commercial airline to hire an African American pilot.
- Launched the first GLBT (gay, lesbian, bisexual, transgender) employee resource group (ERG) in the industry.
- Reported to be the first to establish a Christian ERG.

**Diversity Awards and Recognitions:**

- 2010 Diversity Leadership Award by *Profiles in Diversity Journal.*
- 50 Out Front Companies for Diversity Leadership by *Diversity MBA Magazine.*
- Honored by *Women of Color* magazine.
- Named Best Company for Blacks in Technology.
- Named to Corporate Honor Roll by *Latin Business* magazine.
- DiversityInc Top 50 Award: 2002, 2010.
- And many more.

# Elizabeth A. Campbell

## Partner and Chief Diversity Officer, Andrews Kurth, LLP

 Elizabeth Campbell's work with diversity and inclusion includes a long and personal awareness of the impact of the Civil Rights era. Though she doesn't feel that she was "called" to get involved in this kind of work, per se, her upbringing, the challenges she faced, and the accomplishments she achieved helped her to realize that her background positioned her to have a positive impact on others who were attempting to carve their own path through life.

Growing up in New Jersey during the earliest stages of the Civil Rights era, Elizabeth recalls experiencing overt discrimination and was impacted by comments from detractors that said she couldn't be a lawyer. The people who were telling her these things were not neighbors or peers; they were her educators and advisors, those who were meant to inspire and support young burgeoning talent such as hers.

But instead of allowing others to keep her dreams from coming true, Elizabeth took their lack of support as a challenge—and used it to press forward with her dreams and aspirations. As a young woman, Elizabeth was amazed that there were people in the world who not only failed to encourage others to become their best but in fact attempted to *undermine* their confidence and hinder their abilities to move ahead in life. Elizabeth turned this on its head, however, and used it as encouragement to apply to and eventually attend Princeton University and Michigan Law School. Today, she views the naysayers as catalysts for her success.

In her previous work for Aramark, and now for Andrews Kurth, LLP, Elizabeth realized that her life history—the path that brought her to this point in time—might serve as a positive influence for other people. She pondered the notion that people may not get a chance to succeed if they aren't told that their differences—the things that make them unique—are valued. Elizabeth truly believes that celebrating people's differences makes far more of a difference than merely "not discriminating."

This is the very tenet of proactive inclusion that Elizabeth has built into the diversity and inclusion strategic plan for Andrews Kurth,

LLP. She works with the firm's leadership and marketing team to help drive branding strategies. In addition, she is a Community Relations ally who works within the community to help promote endeavors that align with the firm's strategic plans. Elizabeth, an attorney, has worked in a variety of positions in human resources, including employee relations and diversity with several large corporations. Elizabeth has used her past to help positively shape the future of countless other individuals by ensuring that they have the opportunity to contribute their talents in an organization that respects, needs, and encourages diversity of ideas to solve client issues.

Some of the awards she has received include: 2008 Diversity Officer Leadership Award by Diversity Best Practices and 2008 Legal Diversity Award by the Texas Diversity Council. She has had numerous articles published on diversity and inclusion in business and law journals throughout the nation.

### Company Profile
### Andrews Kurth, LLP

**BOB V. JEWELL, CHAIR OF EXECUTIVE COMMITTEE AND MANAGING PARTNER**

- In business since 1902.
- An international law firm with over 400 lawyers.
- Andrews Kurth has a philosophy that "straight talk is good business."
- Offices in Austin, Beijing, Dallas, New York, Washington, D.C., and Houston.
- Received numerous honors and recognitions for several of its employees with regard to their involvement with D & I in the community.

**Diversity Awards and Recognitions:**

- CEO Diversity Leadership Award.
- Diversity Officer Leadership Award.
- Honoree, Ivy Educational & Charitable Foundation of Houston, Inc.
- And many more.

# Ana Duarte McCarthy

## Chief Diversity Officer, Citi

By her own account, Ana's path to the field of diversity and inclusion was unusual. Her life experiences as well as her passion are what guided her along this journey and ultimately planted the seeds for her to want to help others have a level playing field on which to compete.

Ana jokingly referred to herself in her youth as "a rebel without a cause." That soon changed, however, when she transitioned from life in an all-girls high school to a student at a co-ed university. The school Ana attended—Lafayette College in eastern Pennsylvania—had only recently begun admitting women, so there weren't many opportunities for women in leadership on campus at that time. Ana's school was dealing with the growing pains of change at the same time she was. She cites one particularly eye-opening example: The college didn't have any dining facilities where women could eat on campus after their freshmen year. Instead, these young women had to resort to invitations from local fraternity houses with dining facilities. She recalled that the fraternities actually voted on who they would invite to join them for meals! While it posed an incredible challenge for her and her women classmates, Ana was part of the tenth class of women at the school, and credits this particular pioneering experience for her and her peers as being a catalyst for change at Lafayette College.

It can be challenging enough to attempt to fit into a college environment—with its demanding studies and need to forge new friendships and relationships—without having to face even more difficult challenges of being accepted based on your gender. Ana didn't view these hurdles as setbacks, but rather as opportunities to drive change. By the time Ana was a senior, she and her peers had created sororities that had become national. And she didn't stop there. Among other accomplishments, Ana and her peers worked with the administration at Lafayette College to establish dining facilities for all upperclassmen on campus, regardless of their gender.

Though Ana's initial major field of study had been in biology, by her senior year, her focus had turned to working with and advocating for people to improve their lives and their place within it. To that end, she earned a graduate degree in multicultural counseling and psychology.

At her core, Ana is keenly interested in advocating for a fair and level playing field and equal access to opportunities for all people regardless of heritage, background, or any other factors. She leverages her role as chief diversity officer to execute a clear vision for a different and better future for the workforce at Citi. For Ana, as with many of the other Trailblazers, this is both exciting as well as exhausting at times.

---

**Company Profile**
**Citi**

RICHARD D. PARSONS, CEO

- Founded in 1812.
- Merged with Travelers in 1998.
- Earned a reputation as one of the most powerful platforms for financial products and services.
- Reports they attract some of the most talented individuals in the business due to their diversity and inclusion philosophy.
- Has over 200 million customer accounts in 100 countries.

**Diversity Awards and Recognitions:**

- DiversityInc Top 50 Award: 2003, 2004, 2005, 2006, 2007, 2008.

---

# Steve Bucherati

## Chief Diversity Officer, The Coca-Cola Company

Steve Bucherati was presented with an opportunity. As he reflected on his current role, he confided that he didn't exactly choose this area of expertise. He admitted that he was instead "drafted." After the year 2000—when The Coca-Cola Company settled a highly publicized class action lawsuit alleging racial discrimination—the company agreed to make sweeping changes to their human resources policies and procedures. They turned to Steve Bucherati to lead this significant cultural transformation.

As Steve related his story to us, he indicated that his selection to lead this effort initially puzzled him and he wasn't certain why he had been chosen. He was both happy in his current job and thought he possessed absolutely no foundation upon which to lead a diversity and inclusion function. Being a White male, he initially thought that he had no experiences of bias or prejudice and didn't have to deal with any of the same experiences that many underrepresented group members had dealt with. But as Steve began to do this work, he reconnected with several of his past experiences. One in particular stood out for him. As a young man, he was the only White basketball player on an otherwise predominately Black competitive traveling basketball team. Steve credits this experience in particular and the lessons he learned along the way around fairness as the basis for some of the pivotal work he has led at The Coca-Cola Company where he strives to foster a culture of fairness and inclusion.

Steve Bucherati is passionate about his work as a chief diversity officer. He strives for a more inclusive culture, improved engagement, and a culture of fairness with opportunities for advancement for all. He, like others in his role, truly sees the opportunity and the gains for the people of The Coca-Cola Company that come about when you treat all people with fairness and respect.

---

### Company Profile
### The Coca-Cola Company

**MUHTAR KENT, CEO**

- Founded in 1886, The Coca-Cola Company is based in Atlanta, Georgia.
- The world's largest beverage company.
- It's most famous product, Coca-Cola, was invented by pharmacist John Stith Pemberton in 1886.
- Currently offers almost 400 brands in over 200 countries.
- Serves over 1.6 billion servings per day.

*(continued)*

*(continued)*

**Diversity Awards and Recognitions:**

- DiversityInc Top 50 Award: 2003, 2004, 2005, 2006, 2007, 2010.
- Top 40 Best Companies for Diversity, *Black Enterprise* magazine 2009.
- America's Top Organizations for Multicultural Business Opportunities, DiversityBusiness.com 2009.
- And many more.

# Gilbert "Gil" F. Casellas

## Vice President—Corporate Responsibility and Chief Diversity Officer, Dell

Gil Casellas has a long career of being a supporter and advocate for equal employment and diversity and inclusion. His rich history of efforts in this field have included positions as the Chairman of the Equal Employment Opportunity Commission, and a partner in a major law firm before joining Dell. Having attended segregated schools in the South as a youth, Gil was exposed to the issues of bias and prejudice at an early age. As the son of immigrant workers who did not speak English, Gil understood early in life the importance of the concepts of inclusion and exclusion as applied to himself and so many others.

Gil recalls that many of his relatives were actively involved with the National Association for the Advancement of Colored People (NAACP) and the League of United Latin American Citizens (LULAC) during the height of the Civil Rights movement. His exposure to these movements helped him realize the opportunities and experiences that could be available to all people. His subsequent and later involvement in diversity and inclusion, then, was a matter of natural progression. Once he finished law school, he became involved in many organized bar activities that later included the formation of, and becoming President of, the Hispanic National Bar Association.

As Gil, the only person of color, began work for one of the largest law firms in Philadelphia, his advocacy led him to become actively engaged in hiring matters as he strived to consistently make a difference for his firm by reflecting a core set of values of diversity and inclusion.

In 1993, President Clinton appointed Gil as General Counsel of the Air Force. Many are aware how former President Clinton was determined to create what was then the most diverse and inclusive administration that represented the people of the United States. Gil's boss, the Secretary of the Air Force, was the first woman in history to be named to that post.

During his time as General Counsel, Gil was asked to serve as Chairman of the Equal Employment Opportunity Commission, where he served for three and a half years. In this role, Gil was the chief enforcer of workplace antidiscrimination laws. In this role, he was the driving force and enforcer of equal employment opportunity for the American workforce. His legal acumen combined with his beliefs in diversity and inclusion have compelled him to continue to impact community organizations and his company as a dedicated, balanced advocate for corporate responsibility and diversity and inclusion. For Gil, diversity and inclusion is integral to the way he lives his life. Gil has devoted his passion to the forward momentum of equal access and inclusion in the workplace.

Gil has been a trustee of his alma mater the University of Pennsylvania for over 13 years and chairs the Yale committee on workplace diversity.

## Company Profile
## Dell

MICHAEL DELL, CEO

- Founded in 1984.
- Is the number one producer of computer systems in the world.
- Ranks number 25 on the Fortune 500 list.

(*continued*)

*(continued)*

- Employs more than 75,000 people worldwide.
- Headquartered in Round Rock, Texas.
- Ranks 8th on Fortune 500's most admired U.S. companies.

**Diversity Awards and Recognitions:**

- Reader's Choice Best Diversity Company by *Diversity/ Careers in Engineering & Information Technology*.
- 100 Best Corporate Citizens for 2009 by *Corporate Responsibility* magazine.
- Ranked number 2 by *DiversityBusiness.com* for Top 50 Companies for Multicultural Business Opportunities.
- And many more.

## Kiersten Robinson

### (Former) Director HR Strategy, Leadership Development and Inclusion, Ford Motor Company

 Kiersten Robinson has seen both the favorable and less favorable aspects of being a person of difference. Born in Northern Ireland and immigrating to Australia while quite young, Kiersten explained that she looked and sounded very different from her peers—and she felt those differences quite acutely. As children can be prone to doing, these differences were frequently pointed out to her and manifested through her childhood experiences in the classroom as well as on the playground. She recalls understanding differences from an early age, and so appreciated that people can each bring something different—unique gifts and perspectives—to the table. This is an incredibly important and foundational element for Kiersten in her work as a CDO.

Kiersten believes these many experiences have had a profound impact on her interests from the broader perspective of leveraging human capital and talent management in organizations. Kiersten explains that she's always taken an active role and been involved in diversity and inclusion—even when it wasn't her primary role.

She believes that experiencing others from diverse cultural backgrounds helps businesses take advantage of the insights, perspectives, and opportunities with regard to customer satisfaction. She's witnessed this firsthand at Ford with its 32 nationalities in Australia alone. Some of her early work involved teaching others how different ethnicities can create a culture of inclusion and foster distinctive experiences and business advantages that inclusion can bring to an organization.

In her work at Ford, Kiersten actively participates in events throughout the community that involve environmental, educational, and youth issues.

---

### Company Profile
### Ford Motor Company

#### AL MULALLY, CEO

- Based in Dearborn, Michigan.
- Incorporated in 1903 by founder Henry Ford.
- The fourth largest auto manufacturer in the world.
- Recognized as a pioneer in workforce diversity dating back to its founder, Henry Ford.
- Some of Ford's earliest inclusion efforts were to offer twice the average daily wage in 1913 to attract immigrants and African Americans into the workforce.
- One of the first companies to adapt its work environments for people with disabilities in 1919, and to hire disabled veterans returning from World War I.

#### Diversity Awards and Recognition

- DiversityInc Top 50 Award: 2002, 2003, 2004, 2005, 2006, 2007, 2008, 2009, 2010.
- Top 10 DiversityInc Award 2010 for Supplier Diversity.
- Diversity Elite 60 Companies, Hispanic Magazine, 2009.
- And many more.

# Ron Glover

## Vice President of Diversity and Workforce Programs, IBM

 Ron Glover's grandparents arrived in this country from Jamaica with no higher than sixth grade educations. One of the principles that they passed on to their children—and then their grandchildren—was that no one elevates their status on their own. No one can truly achieve the personal heights of accomplishment they desire if they merely use their own strength and abilities; rather, they must rely on others and be willing to help others achieve their best; then, all will rise.

Ron strongly believes that we are all supported by others throughout our lives and our careers; he experienced this level of sharing in the community in which he grew up. Ron believes you must give back what you receive, and he finds that belief to be a natural way of advancing about the process of diversity and inclusion.

In his early efforts in diversity and inclusion, Ron worked as an attorney for the U.S. Department of Labor. He was interested in finding ways to provide access and improve opportunities for other people. Realizing people resist mandated change, his idea of "suing people into compliance through litigation and other legal action didn't have the effect" he had hoped for; so he decided to temporarily move to corporate law. Ron decided with the urging of a mentor that he could effect change by helping the HR department with diversity as an insider. He worked to help promote diversity and align HR practices with the concepts of inclusion. What began as an 18-month assignment is now a career move in excess of 20 years. Leading diversity and inclusion at IBM, Ron is building upon the rich history of this organization as he trailblazes new frontiers to keep IBM at the head of their industry and as one of the premier companies for diversity and inclusion results.

**Company Profile**
**IBM**

SAMUEL PALMISANO, CEO

- IBM is the largest technology firm in the world.
- Employs over 400,000 people worldwide.
- Generates sales of over $100 billion.
- Holds more patents than any other global technology company.
- IBM employees have earned five Nobel Prizes, four Turing Awards, five National Medals of Science, and Nine National Medals of Technology.

**Diversity Awards and Recognitions:**

- DiversityInc Top 50 Award: 2002, 2003, 2004, 2008, 2009, 2010.
- Top 10 DiversityInc Award for Supplier Diversity 2010.
- Named one of the Top Companies for Diversity by *Black Enterprise* magazine.
- Company of the Year by The Society of Hispanic Professional Engineers.
- And many more.

# Deborah "Deb" Dagit

## Vice President and Chief Diversity Officer, Merck & Company

Deborah Dagit has become one of the most respected people in the field of diversity. A large part of her passion for this work has come from personal experience. Deb learned a great deal about inclusion and exclusion during her upbringing as a child and being exposed to underlying prejudice from others who didn't understand her physical difference in stature.

Deb related that when she was young, she was treated at Shriner's Hospital in Portland. There, surrounded by other children of diverse and varied backgrounds, she lived for extended periods of time in a supportive environment that felt more like a boarding school than a hospital. Deb and the other children attended school, went to Girl Scout and Boy Scout meetings, played games, and took part in art projects in addition to receiving physical therapy. It was at this time, Deb recalled, that she felt she truly began to develop an inner sense of the importance of diversity and inclusion. Though Deb was attuned to the particular unfavorable language that some of her extended family would occasionally use to describe some of the people from diverse backgrounds around her, she was fortunate that her immediate family—her mother, father, and siblings—were all open, accepting, and inclusive in their interactions with others.

While applying to colleges and universities, Deb approached the department chair at a local university to discuss her career plans. She was stunned when the professor told her she should consider going into the field of psychological research rather than being a clinician. He went on to state his biases when he told her that he felt no one would feel comfortable interacting with her because of her dis*Ability*. Though Deb had dealt with bias and prejudice in the past, up until this time, this particular individual was someone whom she had respected and known for a long time and believed him to be an ally. These hurtful comments forged a persistence and resolve in Deb that has never left her as it pertains to inclusion and diversity.

Deb used these words as motivation to continue applying to schools and was ultimately accepted to San Jose State University, where she got her masters degree in clinical psychology. In her time there, she realized she was more naturally drawn to the corporate world of business than to psychology and psychotherapy.

In her early career, Deb felt that she was consistently being passed over and denied promotions without explanation. This, too, inspired her, and later Deb founded a not for profit organization that helped people with disabilities find meaningful jobs. In this role, Deb and her team literally helped hundreds of very qualified persons with disabilities gain employment and obtain recognition for their abilities and the contributions they could make. Deb reflected that most of her clients were people of color, older individuals, and veterans who really needed the advocacy of her agency to help them find meaningful work. This intimate involvement with people, systems, the government, and other organizations helped to shape the very successful approach Deb uses in her work today with diversity and inclusion.

One of the things that stands out about Deb is that she is an advocate and an effective fighter. Deb was also key in writing, testifying on Capitol Hill, and fighting for the passage of the Americans with Disabilities Act. The day after it passed, Deb turned the page, so to speak, and began the work she currently is doing inside corporations where she continues to drive real, systemic, and lasting changes in the field of inclusion and diversity.

---

### Company Profile
### Merck & Company

RICHARD T. CLARK, CEO

- One of the largest pharmaceutical companies in the world.
- Established in 1891 as a subsidiary of German company Merck KGA.
- In 1917, the U.S. government confiscated the company; it was then set up as an independent company.
- In 1957 the Merck Company Foundation was established and it has donated more than $480 million to educational and nonprofit organizations.

**Diversity Awards and Recognitions:**

- DiversityInc Top 50 Award: 2003, 2004, 2005, 2006, 2007, 2008, 2010.
- Top 10 DiversityInc Award for Best Companies for People with Disabilities, 2010.
- Working Mother 100 Best Companies, 2008.
- And many more.

# Susan Johnson

## Vice President Strategic Talent Management and Diversity Leadership, Pitney Bowes

For Susan Johnson, the idea of diversity and inclusion has taken a shape that was molded by influences dating back to the 1970s and 1980s: a period of time when the dialogue of women and people of color in the workplace was just beginning to expand. This gave Susan an enormous amount of inspiration and hope because of the opportunities she foresaw that it presented.

She recalled at the time it was a combination of her inexperience, youth, and optimism that helped establish a sense of opportunity that this new road was opening up for Susan and others. In her work, she simply hadn't encountered with executives who didn't understand the importance of inclusion.

Susan, like many other CDOs, has found that the CEOs she's worked with exhibit a desire to make a difference for their people, while at the same time improve business outcomes. She believes that this is a sign of more positive things to come with respect to diversity and inclusion.

One of the earliest lessons in diversity and inclusion came when Susan attended a diversity workshop facilitated by Pope and Associates. It was there that she learned that it was important to "care enough to be demanding" as the leader of the session, Merlin Pope would counsel. During this time frame, women and people of color were sometimes still facing overt barriers in the workplace, as companies were addressing how to make Affirmative Action and Equal Opportunity an enhancement to their employment systems versus a hindrance. Susan found that most organizations approached these concepts as obstacles rather than an opportunity to level the playing field and provide equal access to employment practices for all.

Susan believes that over time Affirmative Action helped people get past the notion that women or people of color were not as qualified as men or Caucasians. She continues to believe and teach that all people, regardless of their background, gender, color, or any other demographic, should be held to the same high standards. Though she began her work with inclusion and diversity by leading an employee resource group, Susan's reach, scope, and impact has broadened considerably through her role as CDO where she continues to drive sustainable change efforts.

---

### Company Profile
### Pitney Bowes

**Murray Martin, CEO**

- Established in 1957.
- One of only 87 existing firms that have been members of the S&P 500 since its creation.
- Headquarters in Stamford, Connecticut.
- Manufactures software and hardware related to packaging and mailing.
- Employs nearly 36,000 employees worldwide.

**Diversity Awards and Recognitions:**

- DiversityInc Top 50 Award: 2001, 2002, 2003, 2004, 2005.
- 40 Best Companies for Diversity by *Black Enterprise* magazine, 2005–2007.
- America's Top Organization for Multicultural Business Opportunities by *DiversityBusiness.com*, 2001–2006.
- 50 Best Companies for Black Professionals, *Black MBA* magazine, 2006.
- And many more.

---

# Francene Young

## Vice President for Diversity Inclusion and Talent, Shell

 From an early age, Francene has been a proponent of understanding the underlying intent, motives, and impact of behaviors.

She reflected that there were times in her early career when some of her colleagues hinted not so subtly that she and some of her White women colleagues were only hired because of Affirmative Action—that she, and they, were token hires. Because Francene always liked to understand the root cause of issues, she began to look more closely at these inaccurate accusations and have conversations with those who held a different point of view. As she did so, she discovered that these thoughts and comments were not necessarily based on skin color. In fact, she recalled that there were several well-respected Black male counterparts in management who weren't spoken about in the same terms. Always looking for solutions, Francene had many conversations with others and hypothesized that perhaps the issue of gender in her highly male dominated industry—oil and gas—trumped the issue of race and ethnicity.

To test her hypothesis, Francene related an interesting story of inclusion and education that occurred early in her career. She and two of her White female colleagues decided to explore and address an office attire bias issue with the intent to change their colleagues' long-established perceptions. As part of their "experiment" Francene and her women colleagues wore slacks instead of skirts and heels to work over an extended period of time. They continued to contribute their ideas in meetings and speak up about the ineffective dress code. The women began to systematically address and subtly shape others' thinking regarding a woman's ability to make significant contributions, irrespective of whether she wore slacks or a skirt. Eventually the assumptions about the correlation between effectiveness and attire became a non-issue. Fast-forward. Today Francene continues to be a strong proponent of helping others recognize that inclusion and diversity are built into talent management and succession management practices by her oversight of those processes. For Shell, as with many other companies, it is critical to have a workforce that is representative of their global customers, and the labor market. Inclusion and diversity help shape the forward momentum of talent management within the company. Francene believes people contribute their best when they feel valued and respected, and when this occurs employees win, the customers win, and the company wins!

Francene's passion and vision for change and results have fueled Shell's continuation of fostering a more inclusive company. Francene is committed to helping Shell live the motto: "Diversity means all the ways we are different." Becoming a model of diversity means creating a strong and inclusive work environment with an established measurement and accountability system. It means continuing to develop relationships with diverse suppliers, customers, and communities to help Shell achieve its business goals.

---

### Company Profile
### Shell Oil Company

**PETER VOSER, CEO**

- Royal Dutch Shell is a multinational petroleum company of Dutch and British origins.
- Named the largest corporation for 2009 by *Fortune*.
- Shell operates in over one hundred forty countries worldwide.
- The Shell Oil Company, headquartered in Houston, Texas, is one of Houston's largest employers.

**Diversity Awards and Recognitions:**

- DiversityInc Top 50 Award: 2002, 2003, 2004.
- Employer of Choice Award 2010 Minority Corporate Counsel Association.
- Shell and Cargill Partnering on Supplier Diversity Award 2009.
- Diversity and Inclusion Practices Award, Catalyst 2004.
- And many more.

---

# Rohini Anand, PhD

## Senior Vice President and Global Chief Diversity Officer, Sodexo

Rohini Anand, PhD, is responsible for the implementation, direction, and alignment of Sodexo's integrated global diversity initiatives. While this work is both personal and passionate for her, unlike some of the other CDOs, Rohini's upbringing and life experiences were *not* the catalyst. Growing up in Mumbai, India, she was surrounded by her people; people just like her. Indians were the majority in her environment and there wasn't particularly any other diversity to note except there were marked differences regarding socioeconomic standing or more commonly known as caste standing within that society. Until coming to the United States, these were relatively minor issues in her experience.

After immigrating to the United States, Rohini became acutely aware that she was now in the minority ranks and had to learn to identify herself as such, which did not come naturally. She acknowledges that there is a distinct difference between her experience as an adult grounded in the knowledge of who she is as a person, and later being labeled a minority, versus those who grow up with the label of minority from childhood. Rohini reflected that she was aware that there were aspects of her life in which she had privileges and others that she did not. Being a so-called minority in the United States was a new experience and one that shaped her sense of the impact of being labeled by others. Having experienced both a majority and a minority status, Rohini developed a unique ability to relate to those in power as well as the disenfranchised. This insight helped to uniquely prepare her for future work in the field of global diversity and inclusion.

Rohini is aware that she is only one of less than a handful of Asian persons leading inclusion and diversity efforts in a major organization. As she observes the challenges of other ethnic minorities, her experience as an Asian and as an immigrant have enabled her to have a balanced perspective of the work needed to be done and how best to implement it. Two of the contrasts she observed are that immigrants generally think if they work hard they will succeed; their ethnicity will not be a negative factor. She understands also the importance of the concepts of group versus individual among many Asians and how it might impact their performance. For Rohini, these concepts represent personal cultural experiences, not just something she read in a book. Rohini has also noted that as she works with women in other countries, she has observed that they often do not wish to be identified as women managers or women leaders as this is perceived as a stigma to their success. Rohini's knowledge and understanding of cultural differences adds to her ability to drive results as a chief diversity officer.

Rohini has shared her expertise by authoring a number of manuals, as well as articles in trade journals. Because of her leadership and that of her CEO, Sodexo has been named #1 for 2010 on the DiversityInc Top 50 Companies for Diversity by *DiversityInc* magazine.

**Company Profile**
**Sodexo**

Mɪᴄʜᴀᴇʟ Lᴀɴᴅᴇʟ, CEO

- One of the largest food services and food management companies in the world.
- Serves many private and government agencies as well as schools and hospitals.
- Generated $6.5 billion in revenue for fiscal year 2009.

**Diversity Awards and Recognitions:**

- Featured as Top Company for Diversity by *Black Enterprise* magazine.
- DiversityInc Top 50 Award: 2008, 2009, 2010.
- #1 on the 2010 Diversity Inc. magazine Top 50 Companies for Diversity.
- Top 10 DiversityInc Award for Best Companies for People with Disabilities, 2010.
- Named Best Company for Multicultural Women by *Working Mother* magazine.
- Ranks in the Top Ten Companies for People with Disabilities.
- And many more.

# Magda Yrizarry

## Vice President of Workplace, Cultural Diversity and Compliance, Verizon Communications, Inc.

Magda Yrizarry's upbringing in a poor neighborhood of Brooklyn, New York, helped to shape her work as a diversity advocate many years before she took on the role at Verizon. Magda has used her passion for her community and multicultural upbringing as motivation to take charge of Verizon's enterprise-wide successful inclusion and diversity efforts.

Magda's personal motto—one that she fondly recalls that was shared with her repeatedly by her mother when she was a child, guides much of Magda's approach to the work she does. Magda learned early from her mother: "To whom much is given, much is expected." Magda says she tries to live by this mantra every day.

Before joining Verizon, Magda earned her bachelor and master's degrees from Cornell University. In addition, Magda has worked as Director of Program Planning and Leadership Development at the New York City Mission Society, a nonprofit group that helped students from disadvantaged neighborhoods achieve their dreams of attending college.

During her earliest work with Verizon, and before being named chief diversity officer, Magda's role was dedicated to improving underserved communities like hers as a child, through education. Magda believes that it is both her desire and that of her company's to make things better as a result of Verizon's involvement in the community and workplace. Magda believes that diversity and inclusion are not simply about hiring a diverse workforce, but also about helping the Verizon workforce make significant contributions to the communities in which the organization operates.

---

### Company Profile
### Verizon Communications, Inc.

#### IVAN G. SEIDENBERG, CEO

- Formed in 1983 as Bell Atlantic when AT&T was broken up into seven "Baby Bells."
- Headquartered in lower Manhattan, New York City.
- Merged with NYNEX in 1997.
- Currently employs over 260,000 people worldwide.

#### Diversity Awards and Recognitions:

- DiversityInc Top 50 Award: 2003, 2004, 2005, 2006, 2007, 2008, 2009, 2010.
- 2009 Vision Award by the Sacramento Asian Pacific Chamber of Commerce.

- 40 Best Companies for Diversity by *Black Enterprise* magazine.
- Named a Top American Corporation by Women's Business Enterprise National Council.
- 2009 Warrior Award by the American Indian Chamber of Commerce of California.
- And many more.

# 2

# The CEO's Role in Success

## *Commitment*

W hat makes one diversity and inclusion effort tangibly successful, and another mediocre and seemingly irrelevant—both
internally and in the marketplace? Some observers—both experienced
and less so in these matters—will tell you unequivocally that, first and
foremost, the difference is the active and vocal involvement of the
chief executive officer who works in tandem with the chief diversity
officer (CDO). Second is the involvement of the senior leadership
team (SLT).

Many books written on this topic highlight the importance of
CEO involvement and commitment. However, most authors don't
seem to deal with CEO commitment until the latter chapters of their
books. We believe that this particular area—along with the involvement of the SLT—is so pivotal to the successful implementation of
the strategy that it should be addressed within the first few chapters.
We address it here because we see CEO commitment as an essential
first step in inclusion and diversity strategy implementation. Without
the CEO's explicit and early involvement, few actions taken to address

inclusion and diversity issues will gain traction and be sustainable. Therefore, we might argue that, without CEO commitment, you might as well not even engage the organization in inclusion and diversity efforts.

# CEO Commitment Is Four-Fold

The impact of CEO commitment to inclusion and diversity is four-fold:

1. Observable, behavioral commitment as a strategic business driver.
2. Collaboration with the CDO to drive the organizational change.
3. Communication of the business vision inclusive of shared responsibility.
4. Accountability for expected results at every level in the organization.

## Observable, Behavioral Commitment As a Strategic Business Driver

The CEO's understanding and willingness to engage and challenge the organization's leaders with respect to the vision, business strategy, financials, goals, and objectives are critical for survival. This is no less true for the CEO's involvement with the inclusion and diversity strategy. When led effectively, these initiatives are embedded in the overall strategy and can act as one of a few powerful people-focused catalysts that drive business results.

The tone is set at the top in these Trailblazer organizations. What the CEO says, focuses on, and communicates to the rest of the company becomes the cornerstone of what is measured and thus considered most important to success. While this approach is particularly true with any strategic change effort, it is doubly true in regard to inclusion and diversity. The long-term success and sustainability of these efforts is indeed highly interdependent on the support, commitment, and active involvement of the CEO. Employees look to this top office to determine what is most important to the business, where they should spend their time, and what contributions are valued the most— and thus rewarded.

Ongoing CEO and SLT support—from the very beginning—brings a significant advantage that lends a high degree of credibility and reinforcement to the work of inclusion and diversity. This visible and vocal support not only helps to solidify the effort's significance; it also moves the organization from a possible point of inertia to one where it can gain momentum due to the attention that the C-suite has commanded. Steve Bucherati of The Coca-Cola Company remarked that "Anybody who tells you that CEO and leadership commitment isn't the absolute most critical part is just fooling themselves."

Strong CEO commitment to inclusion and diversity is demonstrated by each of these Trailblazer's organizations. Some observable behaviors were characterized by activities such as:

Holding company-wide **town hall meetings** as the CEO travels to various business locations across the country and the globe, and using these sessions to share information about the state of the business—including inclusion and diversity progress and barriers.

Meeting with **employee resource groups**—and diversity councils, in particular—to learn how their actions were contributing to the business's growth through efforts associated with recruitment, retention, and marketplace eminence.

Requiring **updates from the senior leadership team** during operations meetings and engaging in dialogue about successes, challenges, barriers, and interventions.

Accepting and delivering **external speaking engagements** for national and international organizations, and ensuring that remarks about inclusion and diversity are included in each speech.

Delivering annual or biannual **presentations to the board of directors** regarding diversity and inclusion, progress and challenges.

Chairing key **internal meetings and events with the CDO** as well as attending specific **external constituency meetings**.

Each of the actions listed above is commonly and frequently demonstrated by our Trailblazers' CEOs. They were highly consistent in their actions and commitment regarding their comments on inclusion and diversity. (For more information regarding these CEO statements, we recommend that readers view the web sites of the Trailblazers' companies.)

## Collaboration with the CDO to Drive Organizational Change

Their roles as trusted advisors make CDOs the architects of the inclusion and diversity strategy. They also control any experiences of difference as well as learning opportunities that are afforded to the CEO to broaden their perspective of the many issues related to inclusion and diversity.

CEOs during the 1990s might have been more insulated from these experiences of difference. Their leadership teams were typically homogeneous—meaning predominately White and male. Today, most have had personal experiences through greater gender and ethnic diversity on their senior leadership teams, global responsibilities, conversations with significant others in their lives (grandchildren, children, and friends), and active engagement with others through boards and professional associations. Each of these avenues of exposure provides the chance to experience diversity in the broadest sense. This takes place when individuals can solve business dilemmas by optimizing performance and creating an inclusive atmosphere in which individuals choose to perform at their highest levels—and go on to put forth their most fervent efforts as well. Many CEOs today have made a concentrated attempt to get to know members across their organization on a personal level. They've managed to gain a deep admiration of what it may be like to be a part of their diverse employee population, as well as the diverse communities they serve. They've also come to appreciate their company's culture—both the intended and unintended aspects—through engagement in conversations with others who offer different perspectives and come from different backgrounds. Meetings with employee resource groups/networks, external constituency organizations and professional associations, one-on-one meetings with leaders who are willing to share their stories, and general company experiences have all served to broaden the perspective of many CEOs and senior leaders.

The Trailblazers work in tandem with the CEO to perform another crucial role: Identify, collaborate, and create the measurements and reports associated with inclusion and diversity initiative results. Together, these company leaders keep track of progress—or lack thereof—with regard to the business unit leader's inclusion and diversity accomplishments. CEOs thus are able to track and recognize which business units have made substantial efforts toward line management and other scorecard related issues.

## Communication of the Business Vision Inclusive of Shared Responsibility

In many cases, today's CEOs are quite knowledgeable about inclusion and diversity issues, and they have participated in a good number of experiences of difference throughout their lives—and certainly in their roles as CEOs. Most have become quite conversant and comfortable in genuinely communicating with others who are different from them—both here in the United States and abroad. As CEOs and others routinely engage with a spectrum of people who represent the more conventional attributes of diversity—such as gender, race, ethnicity, sexual orientation, disability, and possibly veterans' groups— they fully expect to learn about the contributions that each individual and group can bring to the organization through their connections and knowledge of their own constituency groups.

Experiences of difference may occur in multiple ways, but there are two we've observed with Trailblazing companies. One allows the CEO to interact in smaller settings of three to twelve persons. Conversely, there are experiences of difference that lend themselves to interaction on a much larger scale, like national conventions with hundreds of attendees who represent a certain constituency. Examples of these larger conferences are women's association events like the Society for Women Engineers, the National Association of Black Accountants; the Human Rights Campaign Annual Conference for gay, lesbian, bisexual, and transgender individuals, the National Organization for Persons with Disabilities, or certain veterans' organizations. And these are just a few of the more visible professional associations where it is common to see observable CEO commitments.

These experiences of difference allow CEOs and participants alike to listen and learn about others' backgrounds, experiences, and cultures—and then to teach their own. For the Trailblazers, these gatherings provided a powerful means of connecting on a very meaningful level through a quasistructured forum. Today's Fortune 500 and 1,000 CEOs are well versed in working with people from various backgrounds and countries.

Independent conversations with the Trailblazers—and other successful CDOs from across multiple industries—consistently lead to the specific topic of CEO involvement and commitment. In fact, it's something that these company leaders discuss with a great deal of zeal and passion. The relationship between the CEO and CDO is often articulated as one of the single most important levers that allows inclusion and diversity to be understood, addressed, and led as a key element of the organization's overall business strategy.

When CEOs are committed and engaged, organizations function as cultures of inclusion. Diversity of thoughts and perspectives remain at the forefront and simply becomes a way of thinking and doing business—not an afterthought. Inclusion and diversity become part of the process for determining the best solutions—*always*. In meeting after meeting, as pressing business issues consistently come up, questions are being asked: "What are our competitors doing in this regard?" "Who else has provided input into this work?" "Who has reviewed this?" "What about so and so? Francesca has experiences and perspectives in this area that we should have the benefit of knowing." "What do others think?" Participants ask these types of questions to actively solicit others' thoughts. They want to hear from those who, although perhaps less vocal from a cultural standpoint, are still quite knowledgeable and have great ideas. Ten or more years ago, senior-level managers didn't routinely ask these questions, except perhaps in organizations with strong consumer brands like Procter & Gamble or Coca-Cola. These companies understood how essential it was to know what the consumer was thinking; it made the difference between gaining and losing market share.

Today, on the other hand, *all* companies are keenly aware of the impact their brand has in the marketplace. Questions similar to the ones listed above are asked more frequently and with the objective of ensuring that the best ideas are always on the table. Companies realize that it's necessary to probe even more deeply for business solutions and results in order to differentiate, define, and increase relevancy. They also recognize that understanding cultural differences is a source of differentiation to the employees themselves—as well as to the market—in terms of providing greater marketplace recognition and penetration. Though select companies and leaders have known this for years, almost all organizations now engage in similar inquiry when testing for the relevancy of their offerings to meet customer needs. The average person today is also better acquainted with these issues and can better understand the interdependencies of our global economies, businesses, and the impact that single-digit margins for growth and profitability are having on the bottom line. With today's tight economics and slowing profits for almost all companies, organizations must seize every possible means of differentiation. When this type of thinking is prompted by the mere fact that the CEO has asked key questions regarding progress with inclusion and diversity in the past or might ask again, then this usually only has to happen once. CEOs have become increasingly vocal in their expectations of how to appreciate and leverage diversity in the workplace and marketplace.

Occurring in tandem with this trend are more frequent requests seeking tangible evidence of the diversity and inclusion initiatives and outcomes from many of these companies' board of directors. On average, these Trailblazers report to their board at least once each year. The meetings are typically held as a means of updating board members on the organization's current progress and to engage in dialogue and educate the board on future trends and implications for the business.

The best solutions are often unveiled through diversity of thought and perspectives. Clients, customers, and coworkers all benefit from and expect diversity of thought in response to the resolution of pressing business issues. In almost every situation where CEO commitment exists, the organizational culture of curiosity, appreciation, and resolve to apply the lessons from a diverse and inclusive workforce take precedence over "we've always done it that way" thinking—this simply is neither an acceptable nor viable response. We've seen many instances where CEO commitment has made a tangible difference. One example is food service and facilities management company Sodexo, whose former CEO Dick Macedonia boldly communicated and implemented metrics for his SLT to drive inclusion and diversity deeper into the organization. Combined with supporting infrastructure—communications, education, accountability, and metrics—CEO commitment has created awareness that has raised the perceived importance of inclusion and diversity as a strategic business imperative—one that provides tangible results for organizations.

But what is it about the engagement of the CEO him- or herself that makes such a considerable difference? Some noted authorities on change indicate that successful enterprise-wide transformation occurs when as many as "perhaps 75 percent of management overall, and virtually all of the top executives . . . believe that considerable change is absolutely essential."[1] Our Trailblazers clearly believe that the business reasons and customer issues that support inclusion and diversity were indisputably the best means to promote advancement for these efforts. The days of framing inclusion and diversity as the "right thing to do" have gone by the wayside for the Trailblazers' companies, and rightly so. It's not that Trailblazers and their CEOs no longer believe this to be true, it's simply that the economics of running a business don't allow for such an altruistic approach. Businesses must show relevancy and urgency to make the change that's needed to align inclusion and diversity with the business strategy—and to align minds, hearts, and behaviors with bottom-line results.

## Accountability for Expected Results at Every Level in the Organization

CEO commitment takes many forms. It frequently comes from the CEO's own expectations of better results from leaders and connects to what employees believe about their workplace. It comes from their SLT's supervision—specifically with regard to aggressively monitoring inclusion and diversity's overall progress. Ron Glover, Vice President of Diversity and Work Force Programs for the IBM Corporation, shared the following story with us. About a year ago, IBM was holding a two-day diversity strategy session where leaders from all over the world convened. This meeting represented the kickoff of the diversity strategy that the SLT had just developed and reinforced. CEO Sam Palmisano joined the group to spend some time, speak with them, and then close the session.

According to Glover, "Palmisano was supposed to spend about an hour to do the close—and wound up spending one and one-half hours until finally his assistant came in and told him that he had three customers that had been waiting for fifteen minutes and he had to go talk to them. It wasn't just a speech to him. While he did talk for about ten minutes . . . part of his presentation was an engaged open dialogue with the people in the room— that included some of his direct reports right down to first level managers—who had been diversity champions who we brought in from around the world to help us do this work."

Coca-Cola North America's Group Director of Diversity & Fairness, Steve Bucherati, related that North America CEO Sandy Douglas and his team "facilitated fifteen Diversity Roundtables across the country in 2009, and will likely conduct thirty sessions in

2010." These sessions are designed around six key questions that are posed to the 10 to 12 participating employees. During these dynamic dialogue sessions, the CEO and his team actively talk with participants about the progress and challenges associated with driving inclusion, diversity, and fairness. Executives receive firsthand feedback from employees regarding how well the organization is achieving these objectives. What's also of particular interest is that, at the end of the year, the CEO leads his executives in a candid discussion about what they learned from these sessions. Bucherati made a point of emphasizing that it is the CEO—not he, the CDO—who leads this discussion. Then, together, the two take the next step to determine which objectives should take priority in the upcoming year. The fact that the CEO is the one pushing for an effective inclusion and diversity strategy is incredibly significant.

The message here is that the CEO wants to make it clear that he is paying personal attention to inclusion and diversity efforts. This degree of top-level accountability for results is mirrored by other Trailblazer CEOs as well.

## Commitment Signals Importance

This personal involvement, storytelling, listening, learning, and willingness to engage firsthand increases the CEO's connection to the workforce. In turn, it connects employees to their CEO and leadership team. Employees appreciate the opportunity they've been granted to influence inclusion strategy directly through these sessions. In addition, the CEO and his or her team are very involved in influencing the strategic execution of inclusion and diversity via these sessions. The executive team is often more than happy to have the chance to share and lead with their own stories and experiences of difference. In all, these sessions foster an atmosphere of openness, two-way sharing, and focus regarding inclusion and diversity progress. These venues allow the CEO and the SLT to make direct and incontrovertible statements about the importance of inclusion by virtue of the time they're spending and their personal involvement. In other words, they walk the walk *and* talk the talk.

The Trailblazers we interviewed confirmed that visible commitment at the highest levels of the organization signals the importance of inclusion and diversity throughout. It also implies how these initiatives are linked to the business strategy and promise of what a more inclusive culture is expected to bring to the organization. That the CEO and SLT are committed to this program is likely to be perceived as *the most important factor* in its eventual success—as Bucherati of The Coca-Cola Company would point out. For Bucherati, $(D + I)$ $F = Success$ (i.e., diversity plus inclusion multiplied by fairness equals success). Coca-Cola is on to something here, even if it's just a possible result of their highly publicized 2000 lawsuit. From this work, and that of a court-appointed high-profile diversity council, they have seemingly instilled the essence of a diverse and inclusive culture within their organization. They have learned how valuable it is to correlate their people's perceptions of workplace fairness and respect to an inclusive culture. Imagine that.

To further underscore the importance of CEO commitment and SLT engagement regarding inclusion and diversity, IBM's Glover recalled a conversation with a colleague on the senior leadership team. They were reviewing internal candidate slates for "executive level opportunities" when Ron made a remark about the colleague's diligence in asking a number of questions regarding the candidate slate. As Glover tells the story, he says his colleague looked at him and said: "I'm not doing this for diversity, Ron. I'm doing this because that's one of the ways I assess whether the slate has absolutely the best people on it. When it's not diverse, it's a tip-off to me that somehow or another we didn't get the right names of people on the slate."

There is no substitute for SLT engagement and CEO commitment to drive tangible outcomes—in this case, for results regarding advancement. IBM—known to have a long-term penchant for talent identification and development—believes that tangible actions reinforce the assertion that the "tone is set at the top."

Some of the other factors for success that the Trailblazers discussed included the availability of resources, projections about growth and profitability of the company, marketplace demands, and capabilities of other persons involved in leading change efforts.

No conversation regarding CEO commitment can conclude without discussing the merits—and necessity—of accountability. Inclusion and diversity efforts rise and fall on the CEO's commitment *and* demand for accountability of results.

Over the years, we've witnessed or had the privilege of implementing inclusion and diversity strategies for some of the best-run organizations in the world. We've experienced the difference it makes when the CEO personally supervised the results—and tied them to an organizational scorecard or the performance management system. We've also seen what happens when a CEO doesn't support or maintain such efforts. Organizations with a direct line of sight between efforts and rewards experienced compensation results that occurred systemically, broadly, and sustainably. CEOs who—in addition to their stated commitment—purposely made these initiatives a high priority and consistently communicated their expectations helped their organizations obtain broader, deeper, and more apparent results.

## Walking the Walk

As a leader and manager, what are some of the things you can do to "walk the walk and talk the talk" regarding inclusion and diversity? We'd like to recommend seven actions that you can take immediately from the CEO "playbook" to begin to influence your culture and overtly show your clear intent regarding these incredibly important objectives.

---

### INCLUSION INSIGHTS

#### Seven Demonstrable Acts of Engagement

1. **Share your stories:** Your personal experiences of difference—as well as stories in which you're keenly aware of being included—make strong statements about how willing you are to be transparent and learn from others. You must "give to get," so talk about your experiences. What did it *feel* like when you were the "only one"—woman, person of color, over a certain age—at a major business function? What was going through your head at the time? What biases and assumptions did you have to overcome, if any, to participate fully? How accepting were others of you, and what did that do for you? What did you learn about yourself?

2. **Become an active mentor:** Get to know three high-potential, junior-level individuals who come from a different
*(continued)*

*(continued)*

background than your own. Keep it informal; have coffee or go to lunch. Tell them what you'd like to learn about. Be open to their experiences, and suspend your own judgment. Reverse mentoring is also likely to occur, so remain open to letting it happen. You'll be grateful for what you can learn from your mentees.

3. **Support your organization's employee resource groups** (also called networks and/or business resource groups). Become an executive liaison for the group; or, if that assignment has been filled, regularly attend and support their functions. These groups can be an incubator of leadership talent, so get to know their leaders and nurture them into your organization's leadership ranks.

4. **Make inclusion and diversity updates a standing agenda item at your regular leadership team meetings:** Set and provide clear expectations of advancement and consequences. Reward and communicate progress broadly. Recognize that, when the organization sees and hears little, they assume that nothing is happening, so communicate often to let them know about everything that is indeed happening.

5. **Seek opportunities to include messages of the business imperative and the impact of inclusion and diversity to your company's bottom line in every speech you give and every meeting you hold—internally and externally:** Work with the CDO and the public affairs team to proactively brand your company in the marketplace as an inclusive employer—one that respects the broad definition of diversity and believes in the value of an inclusive and inviting culture.

6. **Build diverse leadership teams:** As key assignments, business projects, and candidate slate opportunities arise, ensure that you're consciously staffing your team with the broadest, best and most diverse perspectives to solve your customer's issues.

7. **Monitor, measure, and reward evidence of inclusion and diversity progress:** Utilize the performance management

*(continued)*

(*continued*)

system as well as your organization's rewards and re-cognition programs to emphasize progress. Recognize the efforts that others put forth in a way that is meaningful to them; and remember that it may not always be a monetary award. In fact, many of the Trailblazers' organizations uti-lized a variety of rewards and compensation. While many of these included traditional year-end monetary and spot awards, they also used more creative means to recognize people—an extra day or two with paid time off, theater tick-ets, a small grant of stock options, dinner reservations for two at top-notch local restaurants, and simple "thank-you" notes handwritten by senior leaders. All of these methods convey a message of respect and recognition for results.

A few additional words about rewards. We previously noted that most organizations favored a reward approach versus one of conse-quences or sanctions, and we were curious as to why that was. The consensus is that change management and cultural change are hard work in general; it's not easy to make progress in inclusion and diver-sity programs. When you deal with people—and their issues, motives, and attitudes—this work can be . . . messy. It's typically not as clean-cut as "Did you hit XYZ financial target this quarter?" The results of this work take multiple quarters—if not years—to manifest through cultural change for the organization. To wait until a perfect score or rating is achieved would possibly mean that many would lose the energy required to continue to drive this work. This is especially true if the behaviors required are not intuitive or if their impact isn't suffi-ciently understood. Thus, providing rewards and recognition to keep these efforts top of mind and ensure ongoing progress is vital to ob-taining sustainable and systemic results. Otherwise, this work would not be worth the effort for some to continue to do—despite the rele-vance of the business case.

The principles that drive inclusion and diversity are not always easy for everyone to understand. To effectively implement the work at an organizational, group, and individual level is more than a no-tion; it takes committed and dedicated work. That's simply the facts of human nature, as many of the Trailblazers—and we ourselves—have witnessed. We offer this as an observation, not a judgment. As leaders and managers, we focus on what we're measured against—period. Deb Dagit, Vice President and Chief Diversity of Merck, added this: "If you have an effective rewards and recognition program, it is also an effective refresher of your business case. At Merck, we found that our nominations and recognition process from our CEO of our D & I efforts gives us a way to capture and celebrate people in different parts of the business that are driving business outcomes. We have a CEO Diversity and Inclusion Award given on a global basis. It has given us a platform for employees at all levels of the organization to not only be recognized for individual efforts, but team efforts as well, and to be able to articulate the business outcomes to the organization."

The Trailblazers' CEOs demonstrate their sustained belief regarding inclusion and diversity through market-relevant and strong behavioral commitment. They are staunch advocates of inclusion, fairness, and bottom-line results. They communicate their convictions and expectations regarding inclusion and diversity every day, in every way, but especially through all the communication vehicles at their disposal. They measure progress, and they get results.

# 3

# Trailblazers

## *Chief Diversity Officer's Role in Success*

---

> **Trailblazer—*noun***
>
> 1. a person who blazes a trail for others to follow through unsettled country or wilderness; pathfinder.
> 2. a pioneer in any field of endeavor.

## Building, Collaborating, Leading, and Leaving a Legacy

It's no mistake that the persons we interviewed for this book fulfill the meaning of the word *Trailblazer*. Many of them have been involved in this kind of work—again, as opposed to affirmative action—for over 20 years, and they are trailblazers in the truest sense of the word. They lay down paths distinct and apart from the old line of affirmative action–oriented thinking and have broadened the work to bring relevancy to other leaders and people—up, down, and throughout the organization and marketplace. These Trailblazers understand, navigate, and leverage myriad strategies to implement large-scale organizational change through the overall business strategy, financial objectives, talent management and human resources practices, marketing, procurement, community involvement, corporate responsibility, philanthropic giving, and the most important among these—the nature of their own distinct organizational cultures. These key points of intersection are critical to the CDOs' ability to gain momentum and advance inclusion and diversity within the organizations.

The role of the Chief Diversity and Inclusion Officer is a unique one indeed. They are the architect of the vision, strategy, and source of fuel and inspiration to power inclusion implementation deep into the organization. A "source of fuel" may seem like a strange choice of words for the CDO's role, however, this very aspect of performance was mentioned in one form or another in many of our interviews. Given the various people the CDO speaks to and for, those interviewed emphasized that the role required the talents of a visionary, advocate, strategist, trusted advisor, inspirational leader, negotiator, and part-time cheerleader. Being a CDO is "not for the faint-hearted" or those who require a great deal of affirmation as a leader. It requires a keen focus on delivering organizational results that influence change and move the dial forward on inclusion of all talent; and it demands that one take a long-term view. As Steve Bucherati of The Coca-Cola Company explains, "Success requires an understanding that you work with the entire organization as an entity and that you understand that the pie of opportunity is really, really, really big. You can choke the organization and yourself if you try to take on too much at once; this is really hard work. It's not as simple as putting in a program to drive sales and you can track results tomorrow. You figure this out bite by bite. Take small bites first."

Many of the interviewees noted that, although this position is heavily people and process-oriented, these Trailblazing CDOs are blazing paths with no taillights to follow. They're laying down tracks and charting new territory with different solutions to old problems, and then guiding others through and over the terrain. While this is admittedly a bit flowery, the point is that without the CDO's ability to connect the dots from various processes to the stakeholders—without specific tactics and the engagement of the CEO and the SLT—the existing people systems and processes would continue to yield the same poor results. CDOs provide vision, focus, and clarity to the human capital side of the equation. The recognition and celebration of human capital gains that benefit customers, communities, colleagues, and the broader marketplace would be far less apparent and achieve much less without the dedicated efforts, oversight, and passion of the CDOs who have taken on this role.

Our interviews revealed that many of the CDOs report to the CEOs—a highly significant detail, since this relationship underscores how integral alignment of inclusion and diversity is to the overall business strategy. It also reveals that each CDO acts as strategist, trusted advisor, and sounding board for the CEO as s/he challenges the organization and other leaders to more rigorously apply, implement, and attain these objectives. Many believe that moving the needle with inclusion and diversity is no different than doing so for other key financial and business objectives. As a member of the senior leadership team, the CDO keenly understands the organizational vision and then translates it into business goals to which inclusion and diversity contribute. Trailblazers set and champion strategy, largely through influencing others to achieve business objectives that positively impact employees, marketplace challenges, and the firm's culture. As strategic C-suite business partners, CDOs influence—and are influenced by—other leaders with regard to optimizing opportunities and mitigating threats. This interdependency ensures that CDOs remain fully aligned with the business's direction as they address issues like advancement, retention, and development; marketplace branding in terms of talent acquisition and "street cred"; and cultural competency in developing an inclusive and inviting culture where employees feel valued. Whether they have come into their positions from line functions or from conventional senior HR roles, the CDOs play a key role in driving large-scale, enterprise-wide change. In fact, the CDO is often the internal architect of many change efforts. He or she works through and with the active involvement of people like the HR VP, Chief Learning Officer, and VP of Marketing to implement and drive sustainable change. It is in this way that the CDO puts key building blocks and ladders in place to advance the overall inclusion effort.

A 2004 survey conducted by Diversity Best Practices declared the top five competencies for effective CDOs as:

1. Leadership
2. Influence within the C- suite
3. Support of CEO
4. Driving change
5. Results focused

Both our experience and the remarks of those interviewed largely corroborate this; however, we believe that the most effective CDOs exhibit a broader set of competencies.

The seven and a half—yes, that's right, seven and a half—essential *competencies* we discovered were:

1. Business acumen
2. Visionary and strategic leadership
3. Collaborative relationships
4. Influence
5. Large-scale systems change
6. Effective communicator
7. Accountability for results
   7.5 Impatient patience

These factors constitute the essence of effective leadership for a CDO as a leader to drive large-scale systems change. While these items—not in rank order—may not represent *all* the competencies of an effective CDO, they were suggested to be the most important. Our Trailblazers collectively and independently spoke to each of these elements as critical to their success. While the majority of these factors are self-explanatory, many of them align to LEADERSHIP ARCHI-TECT® Competencies.[1]

It is apparent at first glance that these competencies could apply to any successful business leader. And that's really the most important point—they *do* apply to any successful business leader. The difference here is that the overlay of inclusion provides the nuance of additional cultural and behavioral insights that supports the CDO in performing their role most effectively.

Each Trailblazer cited stories of how their own lives and experiences primed and prepared them to take on the role as CDO. Interestingly, none of the Trailblazers specifically sought out the role when they first became involved in this work; they were asked, appointed, or assigned. Irrespective of their backgrounds, each had experiences that impressed upon them the challenges of inclusion in academia, the workplace, and life. These experiences helped them become open to the opportunity to later lead their organizations to different heights powered by their passion, insights, personal experiences, and business knowledge. For many, it planted a seed of a vision for a more inclusive workplace upon which they felt compelled to act.

We'll break down each of the seven and a half factors in detail below.

# 7.5 Critical Competencies of Effective CDOs

## Business Acumen

Business acumen is of vital importance to leadership. We focused our understanding on three primary areas of this trait: (a) an intricate understanding of how the company makes money; (b) who the target customers are; and (c) the ability to influence and help other business leaders engage and be accountable for inclusion and diversity objectives.

---

### INCLUSION INSIGHTS

#### What Business Acumen Looks Like

- Knowledge of both internal and external trends that influence the direction of business
- Knowledge of HR practices and systems needed for successful implementation
- The ability to "connect the dots" in terms of involving and communicating to key internal stakeholders
- Knowledge of external competitive and environmental forces that impact the business

*(continued)*

---

*(continued)*
- Understanding how work gets done, formally and informally
- Having strategic and influential relationships with the CEO and other leaders who support and drive the organization's inclusion and diversity efforts
- Knowing and appreciating an organization's culture
- Knowing the competition

## Visionary and Strategic Leadership

These Trailblazers are comfortable in fast-paced, highly matrixed environments. The nature of their work requires that they take the long view and have clarity of purpose regarding the impact that their efforts will have on the organization of tomorrow. These are highly committed leaders who demonstrate—through thoughtful analysis and communications—the interdependence of various processes to the stakeholders. They are big-time dreamers, yet extremely practical about what it takes to successfully implement sustainable change management practices. They understand that "it takes a village" to achieve the promise of what inclusion and diversity can bring to their organizations' bottom line, and they recognize the importance of making the big and noble goals they've crafted a reality. To not work toward these goals would cause many of them great personal stress. They believe strongly in the value of diversity of thoughts, perspectives, and approaches to innovate and problem solve talent-related issues; they demonstrate these beliefs as they develop and influence others to implement inclusion and diversity objectives. The Trailblazers' energy levels rose as they spoke about making a difference—to the organization, their people, and humanity. They were each keenly aware of the impact of their actions and influence as a leader, and their conviction and passion for what they believe in were almost palpable.

This role was not simply another position; it was an unmistakable opportunity to make a big difference, and perhaps even leave a legacy. For most of them, being visionary is a gift that allows them to directly link inclusion and diversity to a company's growth and profitability. It seemed as if—irrespective of how they came into the role—there was no other work they'd rather be doing.

> **INCLUSION INSIGHTS**
>
> **What Visionary and Strategic Leadership Looks Like**
>
> - Taking the long range and broad view to problem solving and decisions
> - Analyzing the future impact of today's decisions that address future needs
> - Having a strong orientation toward results
> - Anticipating challenges and opportunities
> - Solving for threats and risks
> - Developing and articulating the strategy for others to "buy-in"
> - Mobilizing others through influence
> - Balancing organizational focus with concern for the people
> - Focusing on what's necessary for sustainability
> - A sense of personal passion
> - Recognition of the importance of "street cred"—that the company is respected externally

## Collaborative Relationships

Relationships are the means by which leaders succeed, fail, or stumble. These thriving Trailblazers appreciate that their relationships with key stakeholders who allow them to implement inclusion and diversity work. Though critical, business acumen is not sufficient. When a leader has cultivated effective and productive relationships with stakeholders, his/her ability to influence change increases exponentially. The effects of this approach are often subtle yet very powerful. The strength of these relationships allows ownership for inclusion and diversity progress to spread out from the CDO through what we'll call the *ripple effect*. It's the equivalent in nature of dropping a pebble into a pond; visualize the ripples of water and watch the concentric circles move out from the center to ever broadening distances and reach. This is what occurs when the CDO builds and leverages influential relationships to move inclusion and diversity deeper throughout the organization.

By purposefully engaging greater numbers of people, inclusion and diversity results become much more deeply ingrained and

**FIGURE 3.1**  Chief Diversity Officer Success: Collaborative Relationships

can systemically drive results throughout the organization. This is particularly meaningful for two reasons. The first is that these efforts intersect with so many areas of the business—internally and externally—that collaborative relationships are essential to getting the job done and cascading implementation tactics (Figure 3.1). Second, most diversity executives have very small staffs, some of only two to six people. Therefore, their ability to drive change depends almost entirely on their ability to build and maintain effective relationships both inside and outside the company, develop champions, and influence others.

---

**INCLUSION INSIGHTS**

**What Collaborative Relationships Look Like**

- Being influential, effective, trusted, and respected by others
- Exhibiting a capacity to gather unrelated individuals/ groups to establish alliances needed to drive results

- Acting as a thought partner to the CEO, SLT, and key stakeholders to develop strategies to address inclusion and diversity dilemmas in the organization and marketplace
- Connecting the dots
- Seeking and valuing different ideas, opinions, and perspectives as part of key decision-making processes that impact the entire organization
- Building organizational commitment through demonstrated understanding of the business and effective solutions to address future needs
- Leading with "street cred" (external marketplace credi-bility)

## Influence

Our Trailblazers would tell you that the ability to influence is *the most important competency* in their toolbox, since *100 percent* of the strategies they drive are implemented through others. In fact, many believe that influence is the catalyst to making any progress. It is the skill that motivates, pushes, drives, inspires, and pulls others to a place to behave differently than they might otherwise. Influence is dependent upon and interdependent with many of the other attributes discussed thus far—relationship building, vision, and business acumen.

At its core, influence is about changing behaviors. We believe the greatest attribute many of us possess is the ability to influence— both others and ourselves. These Trailblazers employ influence at three levels: personal, group, and organizational. In their book *Influencer: The Power to Change Anything* (2008), authors Patterson, Grenny, and others cite in their research that people who are influencers succeed where others don't—because those who can influence "over-determine success." Put another way: These Trailblazers influence through thoughtfully analyzing business issues, needs, and motivation. They reach across several sources of influence to strategically and tactically drive behavioral change. Trailblazers are both influencers and influential.

Elizabeth Campbell, Partner and Chief Diversity Officer for Andrews Kurth, LLP, believes that the ability to influence others is critical. "From a diversity practitioner's standpoint, I'm an advocate. The ability to influence others is a multistep process that includes educating people. You can't really influence others to see things your way until you've educated them. Then you can convince them of the correctness of your path. This ability to influence others is not a crammed-down-your-throat strategy."

Trailblazers understand the culture within which they operate: how work gets done, who the early adopters are and must be, and how change occurs. They leverage their influence to drive behavioral and large-scale organizational change.

---

### INCLUSION INSIGHTS

#### What Influence Looks Like

- A keen understanding of the climate and culture of the organization
- The ability to listen for understanding plus persuading others to see broader points of view
- Being politically savvy and navigating organizational politics effectively
- Negotiating win-win outcomes for the organization and its people
- Being quick to recognize costs/benefits and persuading others on how to best apply them for the organization's gain
- Showing others the benefits of making the desired changes a reality
- Demanding, measuring, and rewarding accountability
- Helping others to succeed

---

## Large-Scale Systems Change

During the mid to late 1990s, I worked at one of the oldest and largest retail giant organizations. I can recall having a conversation with the then-CEO about how to measure the success of the inclusion and diversity initiative.

During those times, the company's operations were highly competitive, and visible struggles with other retailers were taking place. Quarter after quarter of losses had occurred in the industry, and many businesses—this one included—were in the midst of a significant overhaul of their stores and processes as they fought to stay relevant and make earnings estimates. At the time, this particular retailer had developed a new advertising campaign that showed promise of appealing to a newer and broader set of customers. They began to focus on signature advertisement—"The softer side of Sears"—to turn their operations around. The company started to shed its mostly blue-collar persona and attempted to appeal to larger numbers and more diverse buyers—particularly the women who account for more than 85 percent of the purchasing decisions in every household.

It was during this period that Sears sold its well-known legacy, "The Big Book"—the catalogue that had existed for over 100 years. This was an unparalleled turnaround of gargantuan proportions among the three largest retailers, the magnitude of which hadn't been seen by most other industries. It was a large-scale systems change by anyone's definition, and one that integrally included diversity and inclusion as a means of tapping into what were then emerging markets. In talking about how we'd measure these components, I recall the CEO simply saying, "Culture is what happens when no one is looking." Assessing people's views on specific questions within the employee survey regarding the diversity and inclusion efforts would be the litmus test to the advances being implemented and let the company see how the people in the organization thought the retailer was doing. Later, I managed to capture that CEO's views more fully in a statement he provided for the inclusion and diversity annual report: "Diversity is an important dimension of our commitment to be a compelling place to work, shop and invest. Not only is diversity good social policy, it is also an important business and competitive advantage—one we will pursue as zealously as we do other strategic initiatives" (Arthur C. Martinez, Former Chair and CEO, Sears, Roebuck & Co).

Large-scale system and culture change occurs when performance objectives, metrics, outcomes, and accountability are aligned and when leaders and employees understand them. Trailblazers engage and utilize existing processes, procedures, and systems wherever possible to realize culture change. They are keenly attuned to forecasts regarding changes within the economy, the talent pool, and the marketplace, as well as the implications for their respective business.

Louis Pasteur once said, "Chance favors the prepared mind." While Trailblazers certainly can't predict the future, they tend to be very good at anticipating change, managing complex, often ambiguous, and informal processes; and making sense of them to prepare their companies for the future.

Kiersten Robinson, former Director HR Strategy, Leadership Development and Inclusion at Ford, shared that one of the key competencies from her perspective "comes back to that change management competency in knowing when to pull and when to push from behind. 'Leading from behind' is important so that the change effort is attached to the business and not to HR or the OD practitioners. It's a principle issue that we have and have seen some real success from at Ford."

## INCLUSION INSIGHTS

### What Large-Scale Systems Change Looks Like

- Keen knowledge of business trends and the ability to anticipate and interpret them in service of what it means to the business
- Ability to utilize current internal processes, procedures, and systems, and modify them as necessary to be more inclusive
- Ability to leverage knowledge of change management theory and group dynamics to engage others
- Capacity for making sense of organizational assessments to aid with strategy implementation
- Ability to keep the inclusion and diversity vision interwoven with the business strategy to drive results
- Ability to create new practices within existing processes and procedures to drive inclusion deeper into the systems of the organization

Trailblazers sometimes act as a sort of Doppler radar within their organizations to reveal, advise, pinpoint, and communicate broadly where pockets of dilemmas and areas of success are arising. We found that these Trailblazers leverage their influence and communications skills to keep the organization moving forward toward its vision of inclusion and diversity with purpose, focus, and clarity.

# Effective Communicators

The achievement of inclusion and diversity strategies depends heavily on timely and informative communications. The Trailblazers' ability to clearly articulate the vision (over and over and over), express their views, and act as a spokesperson, advocate, and champion for their organizations are basic responsibilities of the role. Organizational communications become the strategic tool of choice for our Trailblazers in terms of inciting change, assessing progress, and reporting organizational trends, shifts, and updates to the inclusion and diversity strategy. Keeping others connected and informed about these efforts are all a means to maintaining momentum and energy associated with inclusion and diversity progress.

---

### INCLUSION INSIGHTS

#### What Effective Communicators Look Like

- Architect of inclusion and diversity communications strategy such as the following:
  - inclusion and diversity brand image in the marketplace
  - oversight of content for external collateral pieces
  - oversight of content on the intra- and Internet
  - Request for proposal (RFP) content responses
- Acts as an internal communicator of expectations for inclusion and diversity progress by speaking to leaders and middle managers regarding their role in implementation
- Cocreators of "listen and learn"/town hall meetings with leaders and employees to stay abreast of the pulse of the organization and intake new ideas regarding advancing inclusion and diversity
- Serves as the company "face" and "voice" of inclusion and diversity in the marketplace via:
  - speeches
  - presence on boards
  - participation in trade organizations
  - writers for trade organization magazines
  - content expert for CEO's speeches which include diversity and inclusion messages

---

Though Trailblazers utilize many tools to keep their organizations informed, the least expensive and most comprehensive is the company intranet. Typically, in working with their communications departments, these CDOs craft and oversee the brand eminence communications. They also work with their public relations colleagues to project written and visual messages to those interested in learning more about their company's inclusion and diversity efforts.

Most of the organizations we interviewed have very robust intranet presence. In addition, most have substantial collateral pieces to communicate externally to prospective employees and stakeholders. In our search of their external Internet presence, we found a wide spectrum of footprints—some robust and a few with only a modest presence. Many companies had several pages of content devoted to inclusion and diversity within a few clicks had keyword search applications, and many even had tags. Those with less presence typically had a few paragraphs devoted to their accomplishments regarding diversity and inclusion, which were typically regarding awards and recognition received. However, all of them had some degree of a Web presence.

## Accountability for Results

The organizations we interviewed stated that inclusion and diversity strategies are fully aligned and part of the overall business strategy. Trailblazers establish strategy, and—along with the CEO—measure progress against these strategic objectives on a regular basis. While much of the work carries long-term implications for progress, it is equally important for organizations to identify, leverage, and acknowledge any incremental progress being made. This is what fuels the momentum and provides real-time feedback on measurements; and the results are the litmus tests.

---

**INCLUSION INSIGHTS**

**What Accountability for Results Looks Like**

- Ensuring that inclusion and diversity are tightly aligned and support the business strategy
- Creating and executing the inclusion and diversity strategy

- Defining and ensuring that objectives are granular enough that the purpose, outcomes, and achievement are clear
- Demonstrating how inclusion and diversity impact the bottom line in tangible ways
- Collaborating for success
- Defining metrics and measurements, and then measuring progress through the performance management system
- Engaging in quarterly conversations and reporting to the CEO
- Communicating progress through the same reporting vehicles the organization tracks and communicates overall business progress, i.e. operations reviews
- Reporting annually and/or biannually to the board
- Recognizing and rewarding for progress

CDOs reinforce results through the performance management system. For many of these organizations, the senior leadership team and their direct reports have inclusion and diversity objectives as one of their key performance indicators. The significance of this is profound. Executives who are responsible for managing profitability, product quality, safety, and marketing also have specific "people-related" objectives: development, representation, retention of top performers, and enhanced team performance in service of client solutions (in addition to the typical objectives associated with hiring). In other words—results for inclusion and diversity don't stand alone; they are embedded into these executives' overall objectives. Many of these Trailblazer organizations also have metrics associated with supplier diversity spend for products and services with major vendors and second tier spend. Inclusion and diversity have become integrated into the business systems and processes as a component to be tracked and measured. The significance is this—"What gets measured gets done."

Verizon's multilingual, multifaceted business strategy rests with "keep the customer first." VP of Workplace Culture, Diversity and Compliance for Verizon, Magda Yrizarry, put it this way: "At Verizon, we serve a broad and diverse base of consumers and businesses. We have universal principles that support our business. At the end of the day, we believe you can't separate diversity and inclusion from the business. Every person is accountable—suppliers, employees, leaders—for how we participate in the market, drive market share, and deploy our technology. We inspect what we expect; so we take every opportunity to tie diversity and inclusion to our core business."

When leaders are accountable, progress is made. Period.

Effective business leaders demand the same kind of results for inclusion and diversity that they do with other business objectives. However, because these initiatives are so visible at the senior-most levels, the progress associated with them may in fact be subject to greater scrutiny—as there is a strong desire to know that improvements are being made as soon as possible.

In a subsequent chapter, we'll address how the Trailblazers track and monitor progress through the use of key performance indicators, scorecards, and other means.

## Impatient Patience

We recognized that we've coined a new term and feel it is very appropriate to this work. While there is certainly short-term low-hanging fruit to be reaped, for the greater part, this work requires a view for long-term results. Large-scale systems change is said to take between eight and ten years to be fully embedded into an organization's culture. In today's businesses, that's just too long. Sustainable results need to be delivered sooner in order to justify resources and budgets to drive more results. Our world today is marked by restructurings, downsizings, transformations, business process engineering, re-engineering, mergers—pick your favorite business challenge. They are all very real and these challenges are not likely to be eliminated or reduced much in the foreseeable future. Organizations that have already been doing more with less, particularly post 9/11, continue to push for doing still more with less. As our economy is trying to gain some semblance of stability in very uncertain times, all bets are off as to when stability will occur, and, when it does occur, we will likely only be able to know that from looking in the rearview mirror. The macroeconomic forces that are in play during our global economic slow-down have certainly touched every business organization and every person in a very personal way over the last few years.

That being said, some organizations have been abl_____
certain amount of constructive tension and have been able ____
inclusion and diversity efforts even in this difficult economic climate.
We would submit that the answer to their commitment is in large part
due to the long-term views and the importance these organizations
and their CEOs place on inclusion and diversity. For these organizations inclusion and diversity are not only for prosperous times, but in
fact the true measure of commitment is how they continue to address
these issues during the more difficult times. These organizations
subscribe to what we call *impatient patience*.

They are not satisfied with the status quo—ever. These organizations recognize that inclusion and diversity require commitment for the long haul, and, while fully invested in the long haul
and staying the course, they also recognize that there are practices
and efforts that can yield shorter term results today when sustained
focus and commitment are applied. There's a strong sense within
these organizations that doing the minimum and achieving only
that which is easiest to achieve is not sufficient. There's a relentless
pressure for results and accountability to do what can be done today in order to position themselves to deliver on the promise of
what inclusion and diversity can do for them in the future. They
strive for greater engagement of their people, more points of connectivity to their people, stronger commitment to their communities, more tangible results from their vendors, and, above all
else . . . more results sooner, faster, *now*.

---

### INCLUSION INSIGHTS

#### What Impatient Patience Looks Like

- Understanding that change management takes time without letting that understanding create personal or organizational complacency
- Refusing to "settle" for mediocre results
- Collaborating with functional leaders when they appear
  "stuck" by helping them increase momentum with experiences and options that can lead to breakthroughs
- Engaging in quarterly communications of enterprise-wide
  assessments of actual versus goal

The contention that inclusion and diversity can position an organization ahead of its competitors is not a fantasy. A focus on people development leads to continued support and resource allocation to inclusion, diversity, and talent management systems. Many organizations learned from previous circumstances—specifically, immediately following 9/11—that significantly scaling back from their people investment strategies, reducing their investment in the marketplace, and reducing their branding presence during downturns makes it incredibly difficult to restart these efforts when the economy improves. In fact, many learned that it required a rather long runway to get these initiatives back on track to yield the outcomes provided before the downturns.

Impatient patience conveys a belief that not enough is being done; that work is not being done soon enough, and that what *is* being done is not BIG and bold enough. A CEO of a major financial services organization was often quoted as describing this state of never being satisfied as the organization being "a self-improvement addict." The condition of impatient patience is to recognize and fully appreciate the accomplishments to date while not being satisfied with the progress being made until highly visible, tangible results are evident. It means keeping your "eyes on the prize," cocreating new approaches to achieve objectives, and not wavering until more gains have been made that positively accrue to the people and to the business. It requires that the organization adhere to its own standards of excellence, which quite often are higher than externally defined milestones of success provided by other groups. But the ultimate litmus test of progress occurs when employees in the hallways can articulate the strategy and share examples of where and how the strategy has impacted them and/or the organization in a favorable way.

## In Their Own Words—On Being an Effective Leader of Inclusion and Diversity

We know that there are multiple paths by which one can become a leader, and specifically a leader of inclusion and diversity. Becoming a Trailblazer, however, requires a narrower path. We asked the Trailblazers to share with us what they think it takes to be an effective leader. They have provided their thoughtful, authentic, and reflective responses.

Trailblazers want other leaders to have a deeper understanding of what's required to successfully engage and deliver this kind of work. Several noted that they have obtained many pearls of wisdom along the way and feel something akin to an obligation to share the insights and lessons they've gained in their experiences as leaders and CDOs. They do this in the spirit of helping others—line management, leaders, and employees—who want to engage and be more successful in this work. Overall, most of the Trailblazers are optimistic about the progress made to date with inclusion and diversity. Not one of them, however, believes the work is done.

To that end, the questions below were posed to each Trailblazer. Their responses are reported here.

## The Questions

What advice do you have for leaders and others who are considering increasing their engagement in the work of Inclusion and Diversity? What are the insights you want other leaders to know and understand about inclusion and diversity efforts and implementation?

(In framing your response, think in terms of advice you'd offer others about themselves, advice about change management, and advice about the future.)

### *Magda Yrizarry, Verizon*
"The world has changed. Companies are leveraging the power of diversity and inclusion in many ways. The ones that don't get this will become the brands that are left behind. Respect and tolerance work both ways between the individuals and the companies. Those who don't 'get' D & I often suffer from a lack of experience. We all have biases. We're all imperfect. That's okay. The question I'd ask is: 'Will you have the perseverance and commitment to influence and bring others along on the journey?' My mother once said, 'To whom much is given, much is expected.' Given our experiences personally and Verizon's broadly, I believe we as CDOs have an obligation and a desire to give back."

### *Rohini Anand, PhD, Sodexo*
"I think this has to be very personal work. It is not just a job; it must align with your personal values. I often say this is where my work and my avocation are clearly aligned. It is about who I am. So when folks

ask me, 'What are you going to do when you retire?' I don't know because this is what I would *choose* to do. This work is about changing an organization's culture. It is work that will benefit everyone, and we need engagement from everybody in order for it to be successful. We need each person to behave like a Chief Diversity Officer—to be a role model, and to be committed.

"The Chief Diversity Officer has to be grounded in the business of the organization so that they're not unaware of the core issues. They must have a strong sense of the business, be business savvy, and have a global mindset—in addition to strategic thinking, influencing, and excellent communication skills. All these things are absolutely critical in order for future generations of CDOs to be successful."

### Kiersten Robinson, Ford

"In terms of competencies—and I'm not sure if this is a competency or a value set—I certainly think passion and a belief in the power of a diverse and inclusive workforce is fundamental. And being able to clearly articulate this in a crisp, meaningful way for your business culture or environment is important. The other core competency that I would consider to be critical is organization development or change management. You have to be able to influence the system in which you work and influence people's thinking to appeal to both the left and the right brain. Diversity and inclusion really *is* a cultural change. Anything you do in this space requires an established diversity and inclusion infrastructure to strengthen and grow.

"Lastly, we've taken a number of cultural change efforts at Ford. A really strong lesson that we learned in the majority of failures was due to the role that we as HR or OD practitioners played; we weren't 'leading from behind.' So the change effort was attached to us—rather than the business or the operations—meaning that it wasn't integrated into what our employees do. It's a principal understanding that we've been able to grasp now that has resulted in great success."

### Michael Collins, American Airlines

"The best advice I could give is probably that D & I is no different from other areas of leadership . . . or business. Leaders should really understand that, if you are going to elicit what I call discretionary effort out of people, you really have to know who those people are, the places they come from, and what drives them. You must give them room to feel valued and have input into decisions that affect them and the work they do. I would tell leaders that this applies to everyone; that when we cite 'diversity and inclusion,' we aren't talking about just males and females . . . or minorities/non-whites. We're talking about everyone."

### Deb Dagit, Merck

"One thing that I've learned is that it's really important to have a career history of Human Resources to prepare for the D & I role. You don't have to be a subject matter expert on all aspects of HR, but you have to have enough of a rudimentary knowledge to engage in conversations with the people in compensation and benefits, and staffing and talent management, etc., who are going to help you implement any new programs.

"Secondly, your business acumen needs to be really strong. It's important to remember when forming a diversity council that you're not only looking for people who 'get' it; you're looking for business leaders who will mentor you. You need people who will show you how to use diversity to interact with the marketplace, drive customer focus, encourage corporate social responsibility, and engage the people in the core part of your business where you create your products. The only way for a CDO to do that quickly is to engage in reciprocally developmental conversations with other executives. CDOs must use these discussions to help others build their skills as a leader to influence others and position themselves to gain visibility and access to targeted development programs. In return, these executives will teach you about the part of the business where their expertise lies and how to appropriately engage in the integration of diversity into their company. It's a partnership of learning and knowing how to navigate the business."

### Francene Young, Shell

"If you really work on bringing together a diverse workforce—and ensure that they can contribute to the best of their ability—you will receive incredible levels of loyalty and contribution. That, in my mind, is what helps a company go far beyond others that do not make similar efforts. You're tapping into so many different sources and so many different views; and in a commodity business like ours where oil is oil, is simply oil—*that* is the competitive edge. When we then lead differently and market and manage differently, I believe we're able to move the company forward. I think it's a culmination of a lot of little things that makes the difference and creates distinction."

### Gil Casellas, Dell

"I would advise leaders that it's not just about attention to diversity and inclusion but incorporating it, leveraging it for the businesses; and that it's not a choice. If you want to thrive—not just survive—this then has to be part of your business approach and methodology. It must be fundamentally integrated into how you run HR, how you recruit, how you market; and again, it's not a choice."

"If for no other reason, just look at the demographics; you'll realize that you're competing against the entire U.S., as well as companies and people all over the world. Then ask yourself, 'Do I have the very best people on my team?' You won't know that until you're positioned to tap into every possible source. For example, ten years ago, I saw this headline in the *Wall Street Journal* right after the Chrysler/Mercedes-Benz merger. It read, 'In the future, there will be no German companies and no American companies, just successful companies.' I think about this when I talk to younger, more diverse folks. I tell them, 'Look around the room—because Michael Dell's successor could be here right now. It could be one of you. Or, she could be in China right now in the eighth grade, and probably is.'"

### Susan Johnson, Pitney Bowes

"I think it's important for leaders to recognize their role in accountability. That people always, always, *always* watch what you do, say, and how you act as a leader—especially concerning diversity and inclusion. A leader's ability to personally reconcile his or her own diversity perspectives with the organization's strategy is critical. They've got to internalize diversity and inclusion based on their own personal beliefs, actions, and vision—in terms of how they drive their business, lead their people, and act personally. So I think it's really important for leaders to decide for themselves at a very personal level what diversity and inclusion means for them. Then they must demonstrate how they want to manage their business and use the leadership style that flows from that personal understanding."

### Steve Bucherati, The Coca-Cola Company

"There are some very powerful lessons I've learned from doing this work for about nine years now that I want to share. There are three to four things that are top of mind that I consider critical messages. The first of which is—it's really hard work, and it takes time to achieve success. If you think this is something that can be done overnight, you're in the wrong business. This isn't a situation where you can simply put a program in place and drive sales volume up tomorrow. It doesn't work that way."

"The second piece of advice comes from the perspective of being a Chief Diversity Officer, and that's this: The opportunity that this initiative provides is really, really substantial. It is a big pie of opportunity around diversity, inclusion, and fairness. You'll choke yourself, the organization, or both if you try to take on too much at one time. In my first year in this role, the organization was coming right off the heels of the lawsuit and we were trying to do too much too fast. I found myself choking, and I believe I was doing the same to the managers here as well. So you learn the lesson and figure out what bite to take first to do things really well. Then know what your next priority is, take *that* bite and do it really well, etc., and eventually you'll get the whole thing done in a way that is palatable for you and the organization.

"The third point I want to make is that success requires that you constantly build organizational and personal muscles around this work. You have to work with the company as an entity, and consider all the strategic, programmatic things you have to do to constantly build muscle. Then you have to work with individuals and help them build their own muscle. The fourth point goes back to what I mentioned earlier about the personal nature and fairness of this work. What I mean is that the concept of diversity, inclusion, and fairness is extraordinarily personal. Every individual has their own definition of success for what they're trying to do—in terms of what diversity, inclusion, and fairness should be—and that makes this work brutally difficult. This is not some mass marketing opportunity; this is a very personal thing, a scenario for which every individual has their own definition of *success*. So while you can use all the metrics you want . . . achievement is still determined on a very private and individual level. Understand that people will feel included, respected, and good about fairness. So do your best to value and leverage diversity, but also know that you can't win one hundred percent of the people."

### Elizabeth Campbell, Andrews Kurth, LLP

"Leaders ought to understand that diversity and inclusion are key components of a successful business strategy. It is not an add-on or the flavor of the day; it's not something you can opt out of. It's reality. I'm paraphrasing Dr. Roosevelt Thomas when I say: 'Diversity is neither good nor bad; it is inevitable.' And all of this takes time. It reflects change management, and cultural change generally doesn't happen rapidly. Diversity and inclusion requires that you build constituencies and engage employees and other leaders within your company. You build momentum along the way, and this group of leaders becomes very supportive of the work. They use their ability to influence others, which is important."

"However, a major caveat for all this is that you must be aware of the fact that there are people who will simply never be moved. You'll need to be able to assess who they are as quickly as possible. Some people will just never get on board; you've heard the phrase 'Lead, follow, or get out of the way!' So you must identify people who will join you as a CDO in leading and others who will follow—as long as they understand where they are going and what's in it for them."

### Ana Duarte McCarthy, Citi
"What I would encourage the people who want to go into this space to do first is—don't make it about yourself. Every now and then, I see this in some of our peers and colleagues . . . people who think being a CDO is merely a great way to have access to the CEO. I see them running around at all these external conferences, on the stage talking and presenting, and I wonder—what are they doing at their company? This is not about a person. It's not about getting your picture in a magazine, or being able to be the one who gives the check. This is about building diversity and inclusion as a business case, and helping it grow. When people don't appreciate the business, talent, and client value with which this position puts them in touch, they lose an opportunity to make the culture a great place to work. *This* is where we start to fail."

"Maybe this sounds remedial, but I would make it clear to others that this is not about *them*. It's about understanding these initiatives, and making them an integral part of one's company. The people who have been really successful are the ones that have always made it about the business, the bigger picture, influencing the culture, and providing access to growth opportunities."

### Ron Glover, IBM
"I'd begin by telling those interested, 'I want you to be clear about what it is you want before you sign up to do this work.' The question I always ask when I'm asked to speak to leaders is: 'Why are we

having a diversity conversation? What is it about your business— and the potential results your firm might enjoy—that makes you want to spend the time, energy, attention, and money to do this work?' If you don't know, you probably want to stop right now and really think this through. Be clear about your motivations, your objectives, and [your] goals."

"The second thing I would tell senior leaders is that this won't work if you simply turn these matters over to the 'diverse' people to fix. If they could have fixed it, they would have done so already! So the real message is to be prepared for partnership. You have to understand that there are things that only you as a leader can be responsible for; and that what you want from [whoever] is doing this work—whether it's a person of color focused on a community/constituency group, or part of the predominant majority—is their partnership. You want them—along with you and the rest of your business's leaders—to actually go drive and define the results. Be specific about the initiatives that will deliver the outcomes to the business, and to be jointly accountable for making sure it happens. This diversity stuff can seem warm and fuzzy, but it's really about our values and convictions. It is centered on all those things and more. You can't manage it any differently than you do any other part of your business; you must manage it with the same discipline and thoughtful approach, make judgments about what to go after, and prioritize on the basis of data and analysis as opposed to raw emotion. Think about what is going to have the most dramatic impact for the investment made. These things have to be part of the way you think about and deliver diversity as leaders."

# 4

# Communicating the Vision

---

Trailblazers know that effective communications are a cornerstone of *any* strategic business implementation—particularly inclusion and diversity. Without a clearly defined and communicated strategy, these initiatives can mean different things to different people—thereby yielding unfocused results. Trailblazers are masters at influencing and working with the natural process owners—the people whose job it is to deliver and be accountable for specific outcomes. In this case, the role for communications often falls within the Internal Communications and Public Relations departments. Through the co-development of a robust internal communications campaign, Trailblazers are able to influence the expression of key messages that focus and align the organization on the objectives and outcomes associated with an effective inclusion and diversity strategy.

It's critical to provide a consistent and clear message regarding the benefits of inclusion and diversity. Organizations are frequently communicating competing messages at any one time—be it new product offerings, the challenges associated with being green, the ongoing need to reinforce safety regulations, and so forth. There are always other equally critical messages that people need to hear, understand, and act upon. Inclusion and diversity especially require regular reinforcement of the benefits. One Trailblazer went so far as to say that, if his organization was not hearing something about these topics repeatedly through their intranet or their leader's remarks, then it was a sure sign to the employees that inclusion and diversity are unimportant and that nothing is happening—even if it is! The adage of "out of sight, out of mind" comes sharply into focus where these efforts are concerned. Communicating about them is a primary means of keeping them top of mind, and underscoring their importance and relevancy to the business.

In fact, if inclusion and diversity messages are not expressed as fully aligned, integrated, and supportive of the business objectives, then these messages will compete for attention with other messages. They'll likely get lost in the process and significantly hamper the organization's ability to gain momentum and traction with its inclusion and diversity efforts.

Trailblazers repeatedly recognize and address the issue of competing priorities in today's environment of information overload. Some organizations even joke that their people suffer from Attention-Deficit Hyperactivity Disorder (ADHD) from all the material that's bombarding them at one time, and that employees quite literally are *unable* to process the information sufficiently and decide which to act on first.

Trailblazers look for synergies to share and advance inclusion and diversity progress. They disclose results as a means of keeping these topics relevant and in the forefront of their employees' minds. To do this, they work side by side with business, marketing, and communications leaders, supplier diversity, and other departments to ensure a single clear and consistent message regarding the related benefits. They constantly seek and encourage that those responsible for communications embed inclusion and diversity messages within the broader business strategy. Trailblazers are watchdogs, advocates, and auditors who are always seeking results. They strive for a comprehensive communications strategy that makes it easier for employees to focus on what matters: the vision of a more inclusive workplace.

Vision is the engine that fuels the communications strategy. It creates the unifying message of expected outcomes regarding inclusion and diversity. Vision accelerates outcomes; it aligns people, values, behaviors, beliefs, and understanding about how the business can position itself for growth and profitability. Vision creates a sense of urgency, the constructive tension between what is and what will be; and perhaps even brings a dose of excitement regarding the potential of a more inclusive and inviting workplace.

Communication strategies are then essential to provide common language and clarity of objectives and to shape organizational understanding of what's in it for our business (WIIFOB). Well-communicated strategies provide the means by which organization members understand and want to fulfill their role in meeting business objectives. When people have a shared accountability regarding the benefits of inclusion and diversity, they are engaged; and when they are engaged, they look for ways to demonstrate and incorporate these concepts into their daily habits. As this happens more frequently, inclusion and diversity become part of the fabric of the organization—and are driven to a deeper, more meaningful level of commitment, implementation, and sustainability.

Inclusion and diversity must therefore be constantly reinforced internally via communications in order to yield shared accountability for outcomes.

## A Variety of Communications Vehicles Are Required

Trailblazers inform and engage the organization on issues, dilemmas, and solutions to inclusion and diversity through a variety of channels. For example, they influence which messages the company will focus on based on the outcomes desired. Noted author and speaker Tony Robbins is credited with saying: "To effectively communicate, we must realize that we are all different in the way we perceive the world and we must use this understanding as a guide to our communication with others." This means to us that utilizing different means of communication is essential to ensure that messages can reach intended audiences in the way those audiences receive information best.

Trailblazers utilize all the means of communication available to them to inform their companies on how inclusion and diversity strategy is relevant to the business overall. One thing they do most successfully is collaborate through the communications team as natural process owners to drive these messages more broadly throughout the organization.

# INCLUSION INSIGHTS

## Avenues for Communicating the Strategy

### INTERNAL OPPORTUNITIES FOR COMMUNICATING PROGRESS:

- Intranet content that underscores the inclusive culture of the organization
- Real-time stories of diverse teams achieving customer success consistently featured
- Contests that provide employees an opportunity to directly share their innovative, collaborative, powerful stories regarding the methods that helped them function better as a team
- Stories of leaders who share their own backgrounds and cite how inclusion and diversity have aided them with projects that provided customer solutions
- E-mail and voicemail
- Town hall meetings
- Professional development meetings and courses
- Group presentations
- Development of turnkey presentations that diversity councils, employee resource groups, and managers can use to engage employees
- Speaking points and remarks from senior leaders
- Presentations to senior leadership
- Annual and/or biannual presentations to the board of directors

### EXTERNAL OPPORTUNITIES FOR COMMUNICATING PROGRESS:

- Leadership keynote speeches and remarks for professional associations and community events
- Keynote speeches at national meetings
- Panel participation
- Co-development of recruiting collateral
- Bylined and thought leadership articles on inclusion and diversity in trade magazines and major publications

- Internet content that demonstrates the inclusive culture of the organization
- Advertising
- Supplier diversity progress
- Multicultural marketing opportunities
- Communication of work-life practices
- Press releases to the media regarding significant events, awards, or milestones accomplished
- External awards and recognition events

Susan Johnson, Vice President Strategic Talent Management and Diversity Leadership at Pitney Bowes, shared the following: "We're fortunate because one of the core values here has always been employee communication. Our Communications folks do a fabulous job of relaying messages to our employees and encouraging two-way exchanges. You can get only so many emails and voicemails. We just had our top 150 leaders together at a two-day conference; so, right now our focus is helping our leaders to be much more inspirational in communicating this transformation we are going through."

Central to the discussion about effective communications is the Trailblazer him- or herself as a change agent. As credible leaders, these individuals' passion, vision, and results influence communications about the organization's future when certain shifts are made. Trailblazers leave no stone unturned. They have an extraordinary ability to connect related yet interdependent work that, when explained properly, provides a comprehensive point of view on how inclusion and diversity support a company's growth. They work hard at making these initiatives' outcomes as transparent as possible at every level so that members of their organizations have a sense of the possibilities that the future holds when they achieve these goals. They understand the importance of incremental shifts and gains. And, while their strategy is to transform the overall organization, they do most of their work by connecting people with information, stories, personal experiences, and results—one person at a time. As one Trailblazer put it, "This is pick and shovel work. You have to be willing to roll up your sleeves and get in the trenches to model how it gets done. There are no shortcuts."

Trailblazers strive for as much transparency as possible with both internal and external exchanges. They actively engage through as many channels as possible to ensure that the organization is both aware and prepared to address the challenges associated with achieving greater levels of inclusion and diversity.

But what Trailblazers do the best through these various communication channels is to hold a mirror up to the company to show that inclusion and diversity *can* make a difference—to the organization, to the people who work in it, and to clients, customers, and communities they serve. They know that shared responsibility drives shared accountability—which means constantly keeping the organization informed of the gap between the present and future state. The Trailblazer remains consistently focused on the systems and processes needed to yield imminent sustainable results. They are keenly aware that members of their organizations feel the impact of inclusion very personally. They therefore strive to ensure balanced communications that reflect both the heart and head in order to gain maximum understanding, collaboration, and results. Simultaneously, they also are cognizant of the different learning styles—auditory and visual, in particular—and the need to ensure that information is delivered on all three levels at once: individual, team, and company-wide levels.

Trailblazers are change agents, first and foremost. They model behavior by articulating business challenges, developing and cocreating strategic solutions, and measuring results. They take every opportunity to provide real-time examples that emphasize the importance and impact of an inclusive workplace as a standout corporate citizen. They speak at town hall, team, and staff meetings; they provide presentations to various internal departments and employee groups to share the progress and expected results of an inclusive organization. They participate on external panels and deliver keynote presentations at stakeholder and professional association meetings. In addition, they may speak at recruiting events or co-present with managers to deliver turnkey presentations that are designed to present and gather information regarding specific groups' perspectives on their own company's inclusion and diversity progress.

Successful Trailblazers have one story after another about how their organization is reaching inclusion and diversity goals. There are accounts of teams who've had breakthroughs in innovation and client satisfaction due to diversity of thought and perspective, which yielded broader and often more effective solutions. (See the Citi story on page 82 and the Merck story on page 83 of this chapter.) There are stories of how specific business units are posting tangible results in the marketplace, and how customers benefit from the diligent efforts of the company's employee resource groups (ERGs). Reports of these ERGs' success highlight the direct connection between their in-depth understanding of customer issues and how they've used that knowledge to accelerate solutions that have shaved months off research and saved hundreds upon hundreds of thousands of dollars. The strong ties that ERGs have to their constituency groups grant them direct access to unfiltered insights from customers who trust them—and readily share this vital information.

Trailblazers have also shared stories of losing business due to an absence of diversity of thought—which then led to solutions that were too narrowly defined and failed to meet customer needs. Trailblazers tell of past instances in which their organizations may have failed to include and retain talented people due to certain "less than inviting" aspects of the culture. A lack of comfort from these employees' particular dimensions of diversity led to their ultimate departure from the company.

Trailblazers function as the organization's conscience. They are a bellwether of knowledge. They capture and share organizational intelligence and are able to juxtapose and align their divergent knowledge and expertise with their companies' "True North", their core values. Core values to which these organizations adhere represent the bedrock on which they do business and treat their people.

Trailblazers care deeply about their organizations and truly believe in an inclusive workplace for all. They provide rigorous oversight to inclusion and diversity goals and results and communicate results frequently with the CEO regarding progress or lack thereof. They recommend which actions should be taken next to propel the organization forward to leadership; and, once accepted, they begin again with communicating the expectations to the organization.

Trailblazers are well aware of the need for internal communications to match what is being said about the organization externally. They work to ensure that the information relayed is both accurate and representative of the results, language, and tone of the business in regard to inclusion and diversity's impact. They don't take this task lightly, and they make certain that the internal and external messages match. There are countless stories of organizations that were less strategic in their approach. Some got ahead of themselves regarding the external marketplace perspective and began bragging about their inclusion and diversity efforts—when in fact many of their own people didn't believe this to be true. These companies were viewed as disingenuous and thereby lost significant credibility in both their current and prospective employees' eyes. Some of these same organizations were then called out in a very confrontational manner on certain highly visible social networking sites where existing and previous employees posted strong negative remarks about what they viewed as hypocrisy.

Trailblazers fully comprehend the obligation to be honest with themselves and their external constituencies with regard to communicating the progress of inclusion and diversity. These Trailblazers and their companies have indeed made significant progress; and, yet, they are not satisfied. They are almost painfully aware that there is much more work to be done. As we've mentioned before, they hold the long view; they fully expect that challenges can be overcome, and that transparency of communications is a key to making greater inclusion a reality for their organizations.

We'd like to share a few additional thoughts before we close this chapter. One can't talk about communication without addressing its impact on the organizational culture. According to authors Frans Trompenaars and Charles Hampden-Turner in their book *Riding the Waves of Culture*: *Understanding Diversity in Global Business* (p. 3): "The essence of culture is not what is visible on the surface. It is the shared ways groups of people understand and interpret the world." The communal meaning of values, concepts, and ways of doing business are all the methods by which organizations express culture. Trailblazers recognize that shared knowledge and language come to life through communicating objectives. Together, objectives and accountability drive the outcomes and behaviors that shape business culture.

Thanks to the Trailblazers' and other key stakeholders' overt and ongoing communications, the people in these organizations begin to see the promise of inclusion and diversity in their culture. They witness through business gains why it's important that they and their colleagues begin to feel personally accountable for the outcomes of an effective inclusion and diversity strategy. Understanding the needs of the various stakeholders is important to delivering robust and targeted communications that help keep inclusion and diversity top of mind and deep in the heart of the organization.

# 5

# Accountability for Results

## Hard Impact from the "Soft" Stuff

The more successful the inclusion and diversity effort, the more likely you're able to use quantifiable metrics to assess progress. Over the years, I've often been quoted as saying, "The 'soft' stuff can have a hard impact." We particularly believe this to be true with regard to inclusion and diversity efforts—which must yield tangible results to the organization.

But, in order for them to do so, systems and processes must be in place to assess whether these efforts are having the intended effect. The easiest way to determine accountability for results is simply to begin with the end in mind. Therefore, we must answer the question: What outcomes are the inclusion and diversity efforts *expected* to yield?

Trailblazers follow a defined process to ensure that any accountability efforts are holistic and systematic, and can be embedded in the organization.

What gets measured gets done; or, as the CEO from a company not represented here would say, "What gets measured gets improved." As with any strategy, metrics are essential to determining progress; this is no less the case with inclusion and diversity. For many years, the only metrics many organizations utilized were equal employment opportunity and affirmative action numbers: hiring, advancements and promotions, adverse impact, and terminations. This became the source of much confusion since inclusion and diversity measurements were almost always and solely defined in these terms—and tightly intermingled with the affirmative action terminology. It became difficult to distinguish between these approaches; and, thus, many came to see these efforts as interchangeable and these concepts as synonymous.

Nothing could be further from the truth.

Federal government contracting companies have mandatory annual reporting requirements called affirmative action plans and EEO-1s, which provide a detailed set of reports about their utilization of underrepresented people. Inclusion and diversity efforts go beyond these reporting requirements and are typically not connected to this work at all. Instead, they are voluntarily implemented by forward-thinking organizations to help them retain their top talent; fuel their talent pipeline; gain access to diverse markets; meet their assorted clients' business needs through innovative solutions; broaden their reach into varied communities; and ultimately win their organization greater growth and profitability.

But the key word in looking at inclusion and diversity is *talent*. It's less about the numbers and much more about the aptitude required to grow and meet business objectives. This concept of talent is one most people intuitively understand and can embrace, and in our opinion—as well as the Trailblazers'—one of the bottom-line reasons for having a robust and viable inclusion and diversity effort.

## It Takes a Village

Utilizing defined and widely articulated metrics to measure inclusion and diversity helps make certain that leaders, managers, and employees determine to what extent progress is being made. The growth of these efforts goes well beyond the CEO, the SLT, and the CDO; everyone in the organization has a vested interest. The success of inclusion and diversity makes the organization more profitable, inviting, results-oriented, and supporting of a respectful culture. As such initiatives have continued to evolve and have been refined, these Trailblazers program their strategies for success through shared accountability at various levels, both internally and externally. They engage all stakeholders—clients, leaders, managers, employees, and their communities and vendors alike—in their quest for success.

It is widely recognized today that talented people want to work with organizations that reflect their values. The Trailblazers are master architects who identify organizational challenges, develop the interventions and strategies to address them, and construct the metrics to assess progress. Said another way: The Trailblazers develop the plan and put in motion the elements to effectively achieve the strategy. Their organization's policies are aimed at optimizing their people's talent.

However great a strategy may be, it's only as good as its execution. Strategy plus execution determines success. The Trailblazers we interviewed utilize a number of measurement tools tied to business integration and implementation. Many of them are universal and can be replicated in the context of your own organization to obtain specific results. In general, the Trailblazers use a set of metrics that they define as components of a scorecard that track ongoing internal and external results. Once collected, the scorecard can be aggregated for succinct, high-level reviews and update presentations to the CEO and SLT as well as to the board of directors.

It's essential that the inclusion and diversity strategy be anchored to the overall business strategy. One way of looking at this integration process is represented in Figure 5.1.

In the figure, the focus for the inclusion and diversity strategy is defined by the overall business objectives and timeline. The success outcomes are predetermined based on the objectives identified.

Typically only three to five inclusion and diversity strategic objectives are chosen each year as part of a multiyear strategy. This allows for streamlined focus, maximizes the effectiveness of available resources, and enhances the visibility of results for the entire strategy. Throughout our interviews, the Trailblazers revealed how they focused on both internal and external levers simultaneously. Examples of internal strategic levers include programs, processes, and practices associated with talent pipeline management and enhancing a culture of inclusion for that talent. External levers tended to focus on processes that were aimed at improving marketplace branding through community involvement and constituency groups, along with robust supplier diversity efforts. If we look at these categories

| Phase I | Phase II | Phase III | Phase IV | Phase V |
|---|---|---|---|---|
| Diagnostics | Strategy | Education | Implementation | Maintenance and Course Correction |
| • Employee survey data<br>• Relevant college graduate statistics<br>• Market challenges<br>• Workforce representation and demographics data<br>• Business planning assumptions for growth<br>• Benefits and policy reviews<br>• Experienced and college recruiting statistics and candidate feedback<br>• Supplier diversity spend | • Business alignment<br>• Leverage points<br>• Priorities<br>• Goals and objectives<br>• Methodology<br>• Timelines<br>• Resources and budget<br>• Outcomes | • Leadership alignment and education<br>• Diversity council<br>• Business/employee resource groups<br>• HR and other supporting stakeholders | • Strategic plan<br>• Metrics<br>• Behaviors tied to performance<br>• Performance tied to compensation<br>• Rewards and recognition | • Systemically embed into systems, processes, and practices<br>• Ongoing examination of processes<br>• Scorecard measurement and reports<br>• Continuous improvement |
| Accountability for Inclusive Behaviors | | | | |

©Anderson People Strategies, LLC

**FIGURE 5.1**  Framework for Inclusion and Diversity Accountability

with more transparency, we see that the Trailblazers focus on three to five primary components of achievement—largely universal milestones that their organizational scorecards use to measure accountability. We've listed a number of the efforts used by the Trailblazers below; these are meant to be representative, not all encompassing. They include but are not limited to such objectives and metrics as:

## Culture of Inclusion

- Employee engagement and satisfaction surveys
- Employee resource groups
- Education and training
- Number of senior leadership–led town hall meetings and dialogue sessions with employees
- Biannual updates with the board of directors
- Updates with the CEO and SLT

**Talent Pipeline Management**

- Total representation of active population—men, women, persons of color
- Representation statistics: hires, promotions, voluntary and involuntary turnover overall; data cuts by level, by gender, by women of color, by overall people of color; turnover gap between women and men; between women of color and White women; nonwhites to White; between key defined age groups, and so on
- Percentage of growth of overall active population; growth for women, women of color, and people of color overall, and other defined and relevant groupings for the organization
- Percentage of women and people of color who are participating in select leadership development programs, and their advancement rates subsequent to participation
- Overall percentage of women, women of color, and people of color in top 200 positions on a year-by-year comparison basis; comparisons with male cohort groups
- Percentage of women and people of color advancing into senior management or officer level positions on a year-by-year comparison basis and in comparison and proportion to cohort groups
- Percentage of business leaders who have made significant progress in contributing talent to the organization through implementing robust people development plans
- Percentage of favorable 360 degree feedback, particularly input from subordinates and peers
- Number of internal and external rewards and recognition earned and presented to leaders for outstanding achievement in inclusion and diversity
- Number of people utilizing flexible work schedules and telecommuting
- Percentage of favorable feedback of participants and their managers of those on flexible work arrangements
- Other metrics

**External Partnerships and Brand Eminence**

- Number and effectiveness of associations with selected constituency and community groups

- Number and effectiveness of associations with selected universities
- Sponsorship ROI
- Percentage of discretionary supplier diversity spending
  - people of color
  - women
  - LGBT
  - veterans
  - small disadvantaged businesses
- Percentage of advertising dollars spent on multicultural marketing and advertising and the yield to the business
- Number of external awards and recognition

The point in sharing so many of the discreet elements that the Trailblazers measure is to highlight as many universal variables associated with measuring advancement of inclusion and diversity efforts as possible. At the same time, this review of frequently used measurement elements also points to the clear need for focus. Concentrating on a small number of elements at one time reduces the temptation to not succumb to "boiling the ocean" and having very few tangible results to show as a result of diluted efforts and resources. When they selected discreet and meaningful objectives, these Trailblazers were in a much better position to show true traction, gain momentum, and deliver tangible results back to the organization. They both instinctively and practically know this and are dogged about setting only three to five goals for the organization per year. This laser-focused approach also emphasizes the need to have a multiyear strategy to certify that the key elements are aligned, addressed, actionable, and adaptable to the changing business needs—and will yield quantifiable results back to the organization. Through careful and frequent diagnostics, these Trailblazers tailor objectives that shape leaders' and employees' behaviors—and thus the overall culture—in sustainable ways. Detailed objectives reinforce the organization's ability to achieve tangible business goals sooner. Achieving inclusion and diversity objectives is a shared responsibility—one that not only demands action certainly from the leaders, but also from all employees.

We've highlighted accountability practices via leveraging processes and systems; but this has also been achieved by using governance oversight bodies. Examples are the external diversity councils like those chartered by the former Texaco and The Coca-Cola Company in the past, as well as The Kodak Company and Deloitte and Touche. The distinction with these groups today versus many years ago is that the Texaco and The Coca-Cola oversight bodies came into existence as a direct result of federal lawsuits. Those governing bodies were mandated as a means to correct past practices of exclusion. Today's business-savvy organizations have seen the accelerated results that they can achieve with voluntarily instituted governing bodies, whether they're internally or externally positioned diversity councils, advisory boards, or whatever name they're given. These governance bodies are not un-common nowadays; some are understood to have enhanced inclusion and diversity results because of their implementation. Companies such as Deloitte and Touche—whose diversity advisory board this author (Redia Anderson) established—and the Council for the Advancement of Women both represent examples of how these governing bodies have significantly reduced the time associated with implementing effective inclusion and diversity strategies that have yielded tangible results.

Another case in point is Dell Inc. The company's Vice President of Corporate Responsibility and Chief Diversity Officer, Gil Casellas noted that one of the more effective ways of delivering on inclusion and diversity objectives for Dell has been to commission a group of influential, internal executives charged with measuring the effectiveness of these related accountability efforts. Like many other CDOs, Casellas found that merely communicating the business case to leaders—who all very clearly understand it at a deep level—"and telling them that their $18 billion dollar a year business needs to hit certain targets" was not sufficient. This should come as no surprise for Dell or, for that matter, any other large organization. In order for progress to be made, there must be a high level of oversight and accountability. Dell most recently created a Global Diversity Council chaired by CEO Michael Dell. The council and business leaders co-established "some goals (both quantitative and qualitative) for our business leaders—which are essentially the Chairman's direct reports—who are being held accountable because among their performance objectives are to help drive progress around these activities and goals. For example, we know we would like to increase the percentage representation of executive level women globally, so our business leaders have that as one of their multiyear goals."

So is it working? While it might be too soon for Dell to do cartwheels and run victory laps, Casellas claims that the movement has the attention and focus of these leaders. Given Dell's bench strength with top-performing women—combined with its reputation for results—it will likely be one of several inclusion and diversity goals that Dell will also achieve.

For Citi the qualitative issue and benefit of focusing on women, for example, is real. According to Chief Diversity Officer Ana Duarte-McCarthy, "We do a lot of work with industries or client groups that look at Citi's diversity. Questions like: Who is going to represent them on a deal? Are we going to be able to bring a team that is representative of what the client is looking for? We have seen some clear business wins because of the diversity of talent we have.

"One of the things we are also looking at is the P & Ls some of the diversity leaders have and their responsibilities. So if you look, for example, at our global transaction services businesses we have women leading billion-dollar segments and these are significant, huge portfolios. If someone like that leaves the company, potentially they are taking clients with them in addition to our loss of their talent. So it's wonderful to look at the business value and to think, it's 'nice to do,' but the fact is that our diversity leaders have huge roles at Citi, huge P & Ls, and that clearly drives business for Citi; it drives our revenue. It is absolutely about the bottom line."

Our interviews provided numerous practical examples of accountability measures regarding inclusion and diversity that various organizations have utilized; for example, the story that former Ford Motor Company Director of HR Strategy, Leadership Development and Inclusion Kiersten Robinson shared: "We measure awareness and understanding of the One team, One plan, One goal, One Ford strategy across the Ford enterprise. When we measured it last, it was about eighty-three percent of our global salaried workforce, irrespective of which country you worked in and what your position was. We measure it, we talk about it, and it's embedded in all our communications and it's part of our learning curriculum."

Organizations are increasingly requiring their employee resource groups (ERGs) or employee networks—all synonymous terms—to demonstrate their relevance and contribution to the organization. These groups must go beyond the important yet conventional tasks of increasing retention and functioning as incubators for their constituency group's leadership talent. In fact, several Trailblazer organizations have renamed what were once called *employee networks* to *employee resource groups*, or ERGs, just to underscore their importance to the business. These groups are expected to provide focus and demonstrate greater contributions, given their unique knowledge and perspectives of their own constituency group. They must show how that knowledge can translate into competitive advantage for the business and better connectivity to customers and clients.

An example of accountability comes from Deb Dagit of Merck.

"Our Asia Pacific group was concerned that there was a higher incidence of osteoporosis in the community of women in certain Chinese communities; and that we [Merck] weren't getting our message out to them as effectively as we could. Our employee resource group worked to run some ads in areas with a high concentration of Chinese, such as in San Francisco and a few other communities. It was interesting to note that the representatives saw that the ads were posted prominently in the doctor's offices. Several of the reps who were part of the ERGs recognized what was happening and came up with an idea. They had the marketing department go through the normal regulatory approvals, and got the ads run in Chinese. They additionally placed them in some local Chinese publications in Chinese. Once the doctors put these up in their offices, things began to change. So . . . the ERGs and their efforts helped us to understand how to reach out to a community that is disproportionately affected with osteoporosis, and needed to be addressed in a localized way to really benefit from our medications."

Several of the examples that the Trailblazers shared provided a clear line of sight between articulated expectations of accountability and inclusion and diversity results. Other organizations purposely intertwine accountability through several practices and processes to advance a particular business outcome. In these companies, the CEO's commitment to measuring and advancing inclusion and diversity was both essential and explicitly communicated. They typically demonstrate this in the same way that they measure other business topics—such as safety, quality, pricing, market penetration, and others. They all were tracked with the same scrutiny and rigor during operations meetings. What is common among all of the examples we heard is that CEO and other influential stakeholders' engagement—as well as clearly defined expectations for results—yields accountability and, therefore, progress.

One might think that with all these elements in play at once—universal accountability practices, the involvement of senior leadership, and the requirement for CEO commitment and engagement—

that advancing inclusion and diversity should be a slam dunk. But *is* this enough? What else could possibly be needed?

## Embracing Resistance

Indeed, there are a few other factors at play here; and we don't think we could do this topic justice if we didn't consider the other side of the coin. In this case, the other side of the coin contains something called *resistance*. But what exactly is this?

*The American Heritage Dictionary of the English Language* defines *resistance* as "a force that tends to oppose or retard motion." Resistance is therefore a natural and expected result of change. In our opinion, it's best to acknowledge this—and then utilize this knowledge—from the beginning. The Trailblazers can attest to the fact that resistance to inclusion and diversity efforts does indeed exist in various degrees in their organizations. In fact, it exists in every organization and surfaces with pretty much every effort to make change, irrespective of the topic: safety, a new product launch, a new performance management system, or a new software implementation plan. You name it—it doesn't matter.

Some believe that the larger the change effort, the greater the resistance. Contrary to what one might initially think, moving "into the resistance" is more effective than doing what one might instinctively want to do—attempting to squelch its source.

Embracing resistance is not optional, but it can often be difficult for several reasons. You must first approach those who are resistant with an open mind in order to learn their perspectives and engage them. To do this, you must be willing to simply listen. And in today's complex, fast-paced business environments, this almost seems like a luxury. But it's not; in fact, it is a necessity.

Another factor to consider—which again, might seem counterintuitive but can yield significant insights—is to try to understand the source of the resistance. What are the reasons behind it? What is the intent? Do the resisters not like the strategy itself, or is it just elements of the strategy? Which ones? Perhaps they don't like the overall plan of execution and see flaws; or, maybe, they don't like you as the "owner" of the process and may be projecting some historical baggage onto you. Whatever the reasons, you have to get close to the source in order to understand what they have to say.

We suggest that resistance be looked upon as a source of valuable information and an opportunity to explore, challenge, learn, and leverage. As trite as it might sound, there are benefits from embracing the underpinnings of resistance. We—and many of the Trailblazers—found that welcoming resistance may ultimately strengthen the overall inclusion and diversity effort. The Trailblazers' sincerely expressed that their curiosity has allowed them to learn much more about what's required to overcome the resistance from the very people who might be classified as resisters. Resisters clearly have a voice and a point and view; and the Trailblazers have found that they almost always will welcome the opportunity to share their thoughts and concerns with someone of influence if they believe they are being taken seriously. By engaging the individual resisters in this way, Trailblazers learn more about what needs to be done to mitigate concerns. They then leverage this knowledge to enhance their overall efforts and even accelerate results.

Though it may seem odd to suggest this—that resistance might actually enhance the outcome—it does make sense. Think of what happens if you don't engage these potentially defiant individuals on the front end: possible backlash, stonewalling, and other strategy-derailing behaviors. Consider this visual analogy: If you squeeze a tubular latex balloon filled with air on one end, the air is just displaced and moves to another section closer to the other end and enlarges and stresses the latex in the balloon there. So can you really afford not to address the resisters? The Trailblazers think not. And a curious thing often happens when you pay enough attention to resistance; it tends to become a source of support and strategy advancement.

## Why Resistance Occurs

Some people—particularly those who have seen their share of strategies hailed as the "next best thing"—have seen a lot of theories come and go. So it might be especially hard for them to get jazzed every time new initiatives come forward. They might have become jaded; and, if so, it is human nature to resist change for as long as they possibly can. They often find it difficult to get excited about one more initiative—no matter what it is or how great it promises to be. This is just human nature. There isn't a willful and conscious desire to not advance inclusion and diversity, or any other strategy, for that matter.

However, among managers and others who are farther down the food chain and more distant from senior leadership, there might be a belief that, unless there is an inferno of a burning platform, "this too shall pass." They will tell you they've seen it before.

Then there are others who, but for the 12,000 other things they have on their plate, just can't focus on inclusion and diversity—right now. It's not that they don't want to; they simply don't have the time. We liken this image to that of literal plate spinners. Some of you might remember the Sunday night *Ed Sullivan Show* of years ago with its frantic plate spinners, or perhaps you have seen the Chinese Plate Spinners on YouTube. Either way, you get the idea of how difficult it is to keep each of the plates that are elevated on the end of a long stick spinning without letting them fall off—all the while moving about from one to the next. It doesn't look easy, and it is not.

The third category of resisters are persons of great intent who *can* make the time but don't have a clue as to how they should begin. We recognize that organizations have many knowledgeable and savvy business professionals who can quickly figure out almost any topic—and then take action. However, though many understand the business imperative associated with inclusion and diversity, confidence frequently drops; and these same skilled managers seem to need a road map to know exactly what to do next. But when they're given sufficient direction, they get things done with their usual efficiency and do a great job supporting these initiatives.

Though we believe this group represents a very tiny portion of the organization, we nevertheless contend that there's a fourth category to consider: those people who have zero interest and fear no consequences or repercussions. They say—as Rhett Butler told Scarlet O'Hara in *Gone with the Wind*—"Frankly, I don't give a damn!" For these characters we say, don't waste your time. Cut your losses and move on.

But in cases where employees *do* give a damn, what can be done to reduce resistance and increase the effectiveness of accountability measures associated with inclusion and diversity? The answer is: Plenty.

In his book *Beyond the Wall of Resistance: Unconventional Strategies That Build Support for Change*, author Rick Maurer delineates five fundamental objectives that can assist anyone charged with driving change, whether it's among individuals one-on-one, with teams, or with large scale enterprise. Maurer calls these elements *touchstones*. The Trailblazers and many of us have used these and similar tactics to reduce grassroots obstructionist behaviors and develop more collaborative relationships. Understanding this approach up front can be quite helpful in making sure that others share their genuine concerns, and that you as the architect of change remain open to hearing and addressing these issues by implementing strategy. Having used these techniques—and witnessing the effectiveness of embracing challenges in diffusing potential derailments—we feel it's vital to explore this topic more deeply. Making changes early on versus later during implementation can significantly reduce potential backlash.

Recognizing resistance, embracing the challenges it brings, investing in two-way education regarding the challenges, and addressing needed adaptations can make a significant positive impact on a more successful implementation strategy. We want to be certain to point out the obvious in terms of resistance; and that is that it is not encapsulated. It doesn't simply show up once, you deal with it, and that's it. Rather, it is likely to emerge repeatedly, despite the best developed and articulated strategy. Both we and the Trailblazers have found that it is vital to expect its inevitable occurrence and be prepared to engage it quickly and effectively to prevent it from stalling implementation efforts. These Trailblazers have been able to successfully navigate the challenges and increase the odds of inclusion and diversity strategy's success by moving *toward* resistance and utilizing its forces, rather than moving against it. When you can work *with* the people who offer resistance most strongly, you quickly learn two things. The first is that each person who is voicing objections actually represents others' opinions or similar concerns. While these other people might hold the same points of view, they are not speaking out. Second, engaging the resisters permits you to quickly discover their intent. You may realize that these seeming troublemakers aren't operating with obstructionist intent. Instead, they may simply be attempting to share what they've seen as problems with past strategies and are willing to speak about these experiences. Conversations with this group often convey that their sense of "been there, done that" is a concern for the organizations' resources and unnecessary stress. What could become significant stumbling blocks for strategy implementation if not addressed might in fact become a potential solution to the very issues they raise—with the co-opted help from the resisters. It's a lesson in why one should always take the high road and assume good intentions; why not involve and include as many people as possible? Strategy itself is rarely difficult. Implementation, on the other hand, can become tricky business.

Trailblazers understand this and take an approach to resistance that is akin to the practice of some ancient martial art forms. In essence, they take their opponent's momentum and forward movement and redirect it upon contact. It's then transferred in ways to move them off center and off their intended target. While we certainly aren't suggesting any physical form of resistance is necessary here, we recognize that these Trailblazers listen deeply with their hearts and minds to understand and respect others' points of view—even if they don't agree with them.

Resisters who are treated justly feel the sincerity of the Trailblazers' efforts and can work together with the Trailblazers to mitigate the objections they originally raised. Moving toward the resistance has huge favorable payoffs to the organization as well, one of which is that Trailblazers have created potential allies where they didn't exist before. Second, resisters can be proud that they're part of the solution, whether they intended to be or not. Engaging diverse points of view is a cornerstone of inclusion and diversity, and these Trailblazers practice what they preach. They work with, listen to, and influence others to address constant challenges, successfully blend relevant intentions, and incorporate interventions to address implementation challenges. This approach ultimately allows Trailblazers to deliver a more widely accepted and better understood inclusion and diversity strategy. Those we interviewed take such actions through unconscious competence; they are simply one factor that helps to position them as the effective business leaders they are.

Earlier in the chapter, we asked whether having the elements previously outlined and used as universal accountability metrics were enough to impact change regarding inclusion and diversity. Based on the work we've seen from the Trailblazers themselves, the metrics they each have in place at their organizations, and the dogged commitment of their CEO, we the authors say, *yes!* These are the levers that prompt Trailblazers to consistently realize essential progress. The ability to acknowledge these elements' impact—combined with that of managing resistance—guarantees the Trailblazers' organizations success through collaboration and accountability for results.

# 6

# Middle Managers

## *Much-Maligned Malcontents or Implementation Powerhouses?*

*"It's one thing to get good at using . . . the big picture at the executive level. It's also great to have people at the grassroots level getting involved in recruitment, community based events, and mentoring. But . . . middle managers are the people who, on a day to day basis, are trying to make these things work. I think we've done them a disservice by not dividing this work up into smaller bite-size pieces that they can come and get when they need them. . . . That's been part of our problem."*
—Deborah Dagit, Vice President and
Chief Diversity Officer, Merck

When leaders discuss the need to implement strategy, the conversation takes a typical turn when the discussion focuses on middle managers: It's unfavorable.

As we've discussed, the CEO sets the tone at the top, and the senior leadership team "gets it." Together, they communicate and exhibit behaviors that underscore their commitment to advancing inclusion and diversity. It's easy to observe their behavior by hearing both their remarks and the expectations they've set for their direct reports. One can also gauge their level of dedication by observing the metrics for which they are holding their direct reports and others responsible. There is a clear line of sight between the strategy, communications, metrics, and accountability for results—and it's called a scorecard.

As the conversation continues, the shifting focus turns to the grassroots level regarding inclusion and diversity implementation. The active engagement of employee resource groups (ERGs) further provides demonstrable behaviors. By observing their work, employees gain entry to lower mid-level strata voluntarily and actively engage within their constituency groups on important company-wide matters. These ERGs are developing greater points of connectivity to other employees and more broadly involving both the organization and their own managers via new ideas. ERGs provide discretionary efforts and intimate knowledge of constituency customers like themselves by proactively identifying and solving pressing customer issues. ERGs also function as a means of measuring the pulse of the organization. They provide a level of authenticity and relevancy of the inclusion and diversity strategy with the organizations' customers, prospective members, and fellow employees like themselves.

Then the strategy implementation conversation typically turns to a discussion of middle managers—a group that simultaneously represents a critical mass as well as a conundrum in almost every organization. Their active engagement is essential, yet so hard to come by. They are frequently characterized disparagingly as strategy roadblocks or malcontents who make it difficult to gain momentum in advancing inclusion and diversity—or any other strategy, for that matter. They are generally thought to be one of the primary reasons that enterprise-wide change management efforts fail, no matter what the policy. And advancing the various levels of complexities that inclusion and diversity introduce is no exception.

When we look at why company leaders speak about middle managers in such negative terms, we become keenly aware that it is their responsibility to implement—not to create or design—strategy. They don't set the organization's vision or policy, and, until they're able to understand it and articulate it, they usually don't feel that they own it. Middle managers are expected to interpret the vision and strategy, communicate them as activities, milestones, and time frames; and execute the processes by which they and their people must act. Successful strategy implementation and its expected outcomes rest squarely with them.

While this in and of itself is not problematic, the fact that middle managers must simultaneously execute and balance delivery of their objectives in their daily roles as they advance yet another strategic initiative can be challenging. For many of them, it's increasingly difficult to know which initiative—including inclusion and diversity—has priority *today*. So it's little wonder that this group of employees may feel overburdened and tend to push back—or may even appear to ignore yet another strategic initiative.

Over the years—and even more so today—middle managers have seen and felt the immense financial pressures of their organizations very directly. Budgets have been significantly and drastically reduced. Human capital resources have been cut to the bone, leaving fewer employees to complete double, triple, and even quadruple the work in an effort to keep up. Many have scant time to do more than focus on the immediate aspects of their jobs and maybe put some attention toward their people. If they don't see the relevancy of the latest initiative, they silently vow to simply keep doing what they've always done. This group of employees can easily recall the many initiatives and efforts that have been announced and handed down to them—and then subsequently faded in importance as yet another new and better scheme was announced to take its place. John P. Kotter, professor at Harvard Business School and author of the seminal book *Leading Change*, in essence says that major change efforts become impossible to implement unless almost all of the employees are willing to make short-term sacrifices to make the change effort a success. Even when employees are unhappy with the status quo, they are likely to resist unless they believe that the transformation is (1) possible and (2) can see the potential positive upside of change as attractive to both the business and to them personally. Credible, frequent communications that are reinforced through the performance management systems can help capture their hearts and minds and keep them engaged in change efforts.

The adage "this too shall pass" seems fitting as a mantra for this group in particular—at least on the surface.

What the Trailblazers have found is that, while it is difficult to obtain middle managers' attention, no strategy—including that which involves inclusion and diversity—can succeed without them. Their scope of influence within the organization—and over many of its employees—cannot be taken lightly. It behooves every leader who is charged with enterprise-wide change management and strategy implementation to appreciate the challenges that middle managers face, and find ways to work with them collaboratively to make their jobs easier.

According to a 2007 Accenture survey of middle managers around the world, 20 percent reported dissatisfaction with their current organization, and that same percentage reported that they were looking for another job. One of the top reasons cited was lack of prospects for advancement. In a May 28, 2008, Knowledge @ Wharton article entitled, "Caught in the Middle: Why Developing and Retaining Middle Managers Can Be So Challenging," author Joe Ryan, adjunct professor at Wharton Executive Education, stresses that communication is a key element for finding ways to engage mid-level managers in understanding a company's new strategic initiative. He is quoted as saying that, in order to obtain more traction from middle managers, organizations must focus on "helping people at the middle understand in more tangible terms what they need to do. This may include more concrete objectives, examples, and messages so that people who interface with customers or run processes understand where the company is and what it needs to do differently."

We believe that middle managers are indeed the "glue" to successful strategy implementation. Ron Glover, Vice President of Diversity and Workforce Programs for IBM Corporation, says the following: "I believe diversity is about changing minds. I don't know if I change hearts. I'm not in that business anymore; but I do change minds. I think if you're going to build an organization where you really do leverage on the basis of the ability to contribute, you really do have to change the mindsets of some people. And part of the way you do this is by engaging with folks."

Shell Oil Company's Vice President for Diversity, Inclusion and Talent, Francene Young, believes that a key means to enhancing middle managers' commitment is to uncover the personal reasons why managers don't engage more fully. "So I make a point of understanding people's personal stories and passions, then I plug them into what I think may be helpful to them from my role as diversity VP. My challenge with employee networks becomes 'Let's talk about inviting middle management. They're your line leaders, they're the future potential leaders of this company, and they're the ones that are going to pull this through the pipeline.'" Francene points out that more outreach is needed for middle managers. They represent greater numbers of people and potential champions than the smaller number of senior leaders who typically get invited to everything over and over. While it's of course vital to continue to engage the CEO and senior leaders in internal events and numerous external multicultural venues, there are myriad opportunities to include middle managers and "inoculate" them with the advantages of inclusion and diversity as well. They impact and influence large numbers of other managers, supervisors, and people both now and as they rise in the organization. As these middle managers advance, they will bring with them heightened awareness, accountability, and expectations of more inclusive behaviors.

For Magda Yrizarry, Vice President of Workplace Culture, Diversity and Compliance for Verizon Communications, success equates in part to understanding "what's in it for the middle manager." At Verizon, it's helping middle managers understand how you succeed in business through innovative thinking regarding the company's broad base of consumers and embracing its core values.

Up until now, we've focused on the challenges associated with middle managers and discussed how to increase their involvement in inclusion and diversity strategy. Trailblazers believe that, like all others in management and leadership positions, middle managers want what's best for the company and to be successful in their roles. When you agree with this premise, then you can shift the focus to what's required to increase the engagement and effectiveness of these managers in inclusion and diversity efforts.

Trailblazers are leaders who help transform their companies. They recognize that their organization's culture must adapt to environmental and economic changes. They work to define and communicate the trends of the future in clear and relevant terms to their business, and they inspire the urgent need for change at an accelerated level with the expectation of dramatic, tangible results.

There are several steps that frame how Trailblazers engage middle managers more effectively in the inclusion and diversity strategic change process:

1. Focus
2. Road maps and milestones
3. The "numbas": numbers and metrics
4. Performance management and recognition

Looking at each of these separately will help to emphasize their impact and explain how they can increase the effectiveness and willingness of middle managers to engage in inclusion and diversity to a greater extent.

# Focus

The many dimensions of inclusion and diversity can be quite confusing and overwhelming; as such, it's difficult to know where to begin. The adage "you can't boil the ocean" is highly relevant in this context; instead, you must concentrate on a few essential components. Trailblazers are masters at identifying and anticipating the most critical issues that their businesses face—both short and long term—and developing strategies to address these. Examples that the Trailblazers began to address several years ago—and have only recently become familiar to most others through the media—are such issues as the impact of four generations present in the workplace today; the effect of social networks and social media, and how work gets done through them; the need to understand "retirement" in new terms (this, long before the official recession hit); and the resultant growing percentages of women in the workforce, particularly in light of the many recent downsizings. This is immediately followed by the implications this has on organizational culture as more and more women take the helm and increase their representation at the top and middle levels of major corporations.

According to the December 30, 2009, edition of *The Economist*, "In America three out of four people thrown out of work since the 'mancession' began have been male. And the shift towards women is likely to continue: by 2011 there will be 2.6m more female than male university students in America." While many of these issues seem to have just come on the horizon for the general public, the Trailblazers have been facing them for four to five years already. These types of significant trends—among others like the green initiative—are matters that Trailblazers have been communicating and addressing in their organizations for some time. While they must still focus on these, many have already moved on to the next set of concerns that will impact their organizations. They are already scanning the horizon with immediate and long-term focus as they work to position their organizations to face future challenges.

## Road Maps and Milestones

Providing middle managers with a road map and milestones significantly increases the opportunities for systemically embedding and sustaining inclusion and diversity in the organization. This simply means that enterprise-wide strategy implementation is often less difficult when you simplify the complex issues and specifically lay out what middle managers must do to engage and succeed in implementing inclusion and diversity. Middle management is inundated with requests that go above and beyond their "day jobs" at every turn; so, in order to increase the mind share for inclusion and diversity implementation, expectations of results must be relevant, focused, clear, actionable, and time-bound. When this is done, middle management readily engages and embraces the inclusion and diversity strategy. In fact, they are often masters at understanding how to translate most business strategies into successful implementation practices for their area of responsibility.

When it comes to the topic of diversity and inclusion, however, a specific set of guidelines and milestones is necessary—otherwise, middle managers will almost naturally default to inactivity. These individuals usually don't feel that they know what to do regarding these initiatives and are even less sure of how to complete the activities needed in order to make progress. This isn't the case, though, if they receive specific directions that enhance their basic understanding of inclusion and diversity objectives and outcomes expected. It's a curious conundrum to observe.

With so many talented people who are known as individuals who "get it done and make it happen" no matter what the task, why this uncertainty exists in the middle manager ranks is a puzzle. While we can only speculate (and we realize the danger in this), we do notice that great numbers of people in this current group of middle managers are largely Baby Boomers. Perhaps many of these Baby Boomers may have lingering memories and experiences of the mid-60s and early 70s that cause them to be overly reflective of past conflicts versus focused on the future gains. Maybe they feel that, as middle managers, they have been inadequately educated on how to develop and get the most from all their people. Again, we admit this is purely conjecture on our part; we don't know of any research that has specifically looked at the difficulties associated with middle management's engagement (or lack thereof) with inclusion and diversity.

Frequently communicated messages and clear milestones that mark the business relevancy of inclusion and diversity allow middle managers—who are central to removing inertia and advancing inclusion and diversity—to become aware of the difference they're making. They can see how they're helping their organizations make progress in the marketplace and workplace. Second only to the CEO, middle managers do more to shape a company's culture than any other group of people. Armed with the guidelines that feed directly into the organizational scorecard, middle managers can become strong advocates for inclusion and diversity. There is a clear line of sight between the work that they do, the benefits to the organization, and recognition of their efforts through the performance management and rewards systems. To the extent that the expected performance and rewards are closely linked, rather than a "bolt on" effort, strategy implementation overtly becomes an integral part of the middle managers' jobs. As key implementers of strategy, fully informed, aligned, and equipped middle managers become central to the organization's success. Middle managers have the potential to become strong allies of inclusion and diversity.

## The "Numbas": Numbers and Metrics

The road map provides focus and defines what must be accomplished, while milestones outline when certain tactics of the strategy are to be implemented. Both are equally important gauges to understanding when and how the organization is attaining goals. Trailblazers actively and confidentially share the numbers with key constituents in order to increase transparency, enhance ownership, and drive inclusion and diversity progress in the same way as other business metrics critical to the organization.

In a previous chapter on accountability, we spoke about the necessity of having clearly defined and achievable goals for specific levels of the organization business unit, function, regional, and local geographies—and with specifically named positions accountable for achieving the results. We know that middle managers live by the numbers. Having a relevant data set for inclusion and diversity makes the difference between driving significantly accelerated strides of progress and simply making incremental "baby steps." Embedding inclusion and diversity metrics into the enterprise-wide scorecard lets Trailblazers infuse metrics vertically and horizontally into all parts of the organization, which ultimately roll up to the overall scorecard. Through transparency, Trailblazers have increased the rate of progress at all levels. It is extremely important for the organization and critical for middle managers to know how close they are to achieving the expected results at all times.

The organizations in which middle managers have been integrally and effectively involved from the beginning have—not surprisingly—made *much* greater progress. In organizations with highly transparent data, managers and leaders are held accountable for specific quantifiable results. They have typically achieved these results sooner because of this shared ownership and clarity of accountability. As a result, middle managers who were involved in the solution early on have engaged the implementation process much more fully.

Trailblazers are highly effective in providing context and setting the parameters around the communication of confidential and proprietary information regarding goals and goal attainment. They use scorecards to track and communicate in an objective way how the change efforts are working and, thus, driving the desired behaviors. Having key elements of the inclusion and diversity strategy embedded into the broader organizational scorecard ensures that middle managers understand that senior management recognizes the importance of their engagement in advancing the strategy. Transparency of results keeps everyone, leaders and managers alike, focused on what matters.

## Performance Management and Recognition

It's been said before that "what gets measured gets done." What makes middle managers willing to take on tasks that drive organizational change strategies? While the answer may be altruistic for some, we haven't found that to be the case with most. Knowing that leadership appreciates middle managers' efforts—and that this will be reflected through the performance management system—is often what sustains the behaviors needed to influence results with strategy implementation. Though most middle managers are expected to accomplish more than their share of work—especially in today's resource constrained environment—they must perceive the strategy as more than a passing fad in order to commit and maintain mind share. Senior leadership must communicate the strategy's business relevancy and continue to drive momentum by modeling key behaviors—which includes recognizing middle managers' efforts. Recognition and rewards are important elements of sustainability for results. In recognizing key behaviors, the change management effort can take firm hold and shape the desired culture of inclusion.

Trailblazers encourage the "stickiness" of strategy implementation through their work with leaders and middle managers. They find ways to publicly share stories of people and teams that are exhibiting the desired new behaviors and the success they are achieving through their roles. Posting these stories to the intranet for the entire organization to read, ensuring that there are updates to the senior leadership team and discussing these instances with the diversity council and at town hall meetings are just a few examples of the ways Trailblazers market the work of leaders and managers who are making a difference through inclusion and diversity. This has a positive effect in spreading the word, and it promotes a bit of friendly internal competition while acknowledging that leadership is paying attention. In addition, sharing information routinely serves as concrete examples of progress that can be captured and factored into the performance evaluations and management processes for the business and business unit/function leaders.

It's important to remember that, without the attention and reinforcement from the Trailblazers regarding the desired behaviors of middle managers, without ongoing recognition from the organization's senior leaders regarding the desired behaviors, and without the performance management and evaluation systems supporting the new behaviors, middle managers—this group of people so critical to the success of inclusion and diversity implementation—will falter and revert to their old ways of inertia.

As we've said, middle managers within organizations account for critical mass. They have powerful norms that will pull them back toward complacency and more of the same. By working collaboratively with senior leaders who model and reward the expected behaviors, these middle managers embrace and significantly engage in change. Even knowing this, however, we acknowledge that cultural norms do not change overnight. With metrics, persistence, an aligned performance management system, and a clear focus on achieving the vision, middle managers can be powerhouses of implementation—and accelerants to fuel inclusion and diversity efforts.

# 7

# Changing the Culture Through Education

## Why Diversity Training Doesn't Work— and How to Fix It

D iversity "training" simply does not work. It never has, and it likely never will. Organizations of all types and sizes have been attempting to change their workplace culture through inclusion and diversity training and education alone. Years and hundreds of millions of dollars later, many have observed that an employee reverts back to previous attitudes and behaviors a week or two after attending diversity awareness training—even though the training and education evaluations indicated the sessions were "successful."

## The Myth about Inclusion and Diversity Training

According to the *American Sociological Review*, "A comprehensive review of 31 years of data from 830 mid-size to large U.S. workplaces found that the kind of diversity training and education exercises offered at most firms were followed by a 7.5 percent drop in the number of women in management. The number of Black, female managers fell by 10 percent, and the number of Black men in top positions fell by 12 percent. Similar effects were seen for Latinos and Asians."[1]

If this article describes common practices within U.S. companies, why then do organizations continue to offer diversity training and education?

There are several reasons, but first let's address the common error illustrated by the above research. Diversity training and education is often blamed for an organization's failure to meet inclusion and diversity goals. Kalev tried to correlate the effectiveness of diversity awareness training to turnover among underrepresented managers. But, unless the workshop is designed to focus specifically on recruiting and retention practices, one can't expect general training exercises of any kind to impact these elements. Leadership must reinforce training concepts, resources, and accountability for the actions taken in workshops to naturally become a habit within the organization's cultural behavior.

While the quote above was frequently used in mainstream media accounts of diversity in the workplace—and also used to further the argument that diversity training is a waste of corporate dollars—a read of the full research documents points to a much more complex conclusion:

> "Broadly speaking, our findings suggest that even though inequality at work may be rooted in managerial bias and the social isolation of women and minorities, the best hope for remedying it may lie in practices that assign organizational responsibility for change."[2]

This statement supports research we've done that indicates the attitudes and biases of management directly impact minority engagement and turnover. (See chapter 12 for more details regarding our research.) Unfortunately, for the purpose of headlines, Kalev's statement about inclusion and diversity training was taken out of context. It served only to derail the efforts of effective inclusion and diversity training.

One of our Trailblazers had this to say about the above research:

"We have mandatory training and education for all of our 18,000 managers. We have five learning labs on generations, micro-inequities, gender, cross-cultural communications, and sexual orientation. These labs are not mandatory, but the demand is so great that we instruct our internal folks to deliver those trainings. Sodexo makes a distinction between training and education that pertains to affirmative action and EEO and diversity training and education, which encompasses cultural competency, outreach, recruitment, and mentoring on multiple platforms."[3]

## Training as a Tool to Reduce the Threat of Lawsuits

The trend to offer awareness training began in earnest during the civil rights movement of the 1960s, but it was actually Equal Employment Opportunity (EEO) and Affirmative Action (AA) compliance training. In those early days, it focused on compliance with EEO and AA due to the increased minority and women-related regulations to grant them greater access in the workforce. Many considered this approach to be a way to reduce discrimination and lawsuits or, if sued, reduce penalties. When legal issues were the focus, the training and education were usually coordinated through the Affirmative Action and EEO office of the company.

The two most famous discrimination cases—Abdallah et al. versus The Coca-Cola Company settlement of $192.5 million in 2001, and Roberts versus The Texaco Company settlement for $170 million in 1996—forced organizations to sit up and take notice. These cases and others like them showed leaders that discriminatory treatment of employees does indeed impact the bottom line.

Although discrimination is real and businesses can lose money, reputation, and market share because of it, this approach—incorrectly called "inclusion and diversity"—often creates a barrier between the educational content and the employees' willingness to learn—even before they attend a session. Majority group members generally don't want to be made to feel responsible for the injustices of the past. Additionally, many minority or underrepresented individuals don't think they need such training, since they may experience the effects of bigotry and exclusion daily. Successfully creating a productive learning environment in this climate is difficult at best.

## Many Leaders Want to Follow the Path of Least Resistance

If only a handful of executives think diversity training and education is worthwhile, their compromise is to offer training and education without the necessary resources to support the transfer of learning to on-the-job behavior and culture change. Some leaders who advocate the causes believe that supporting diversity is the right thing to do whether there are business implications or not. Unfortunately, many diversity champions simply believe that, if they just deliver a half-day or less of a diversity training and education program, they can point to this as proof that the organization supports diversity, and thus, their moral obligation is met. They can then check off the box and move on to what's next.

Human Resource leaders have so many responsibilities on their plate that, when it comes to these issues, the easiest fix is usually to offer diversity awareness training. Then it too can be marked off the "to do" list. Unfortunately, this tactic renders inclusion and diversity a "program of the month" instead of a key component of the organization's people development and business strategy.

Many leaders think the best place to begin this initiative is with awareness training and education. When they're missing a fully developed inclusion and diversity business strategy, training and education appears to be the logical first step. Some leaders see this approach as only about being polite to others. In this case, an awareness program that focuses on political correctness is the only focus they think they need.

As budgets are cut, some organizations have relegated inclusion and diversity training and education to an online format called e-learning, often to just "get it done." While this approach is cost efficient compared to an in-person session, it's not necessarily cost effective. Participants can check diversity training and education off their list once they complete the online course, but if there is no dialogue and engagement with others of difference about the course content and key learnings, both time and money may have been wasted. Engagement and conversation help people recognize—and then respect—differing points of view. Without this element, inclusion and diversity training and education become a limited memorization process. Online learning only has a place within inclusion and diversity education when it is coupled with other tactics and reinforcements to transfer the learning to on-the-job behavior.

While these approaches may not harm the organization, they won't truly change the workplace climate and culture into one that embraces differences and fosters inclusion in order to transform the business's results.

## How to Make Inclusion and Diversity Education Worth the Investment

Our clients often indicate they want to launch their diversity strategy by adding training and education to their workplace curriculum. While it seems logical to start by educating everyone—so that all are on the same page—we actually advise against this approach. Our Trailblazers see the training component of the initiative as an integral *part* of their total inclusion and diversity strategic plan, but rarely is it the first step in the process. All of the Trailblazers interviewed for this book stated in one way or another that their training and education goals, content, and delivery have an integral connection to the company's inclusion and diversity strategy. Training is not the only diversity intervention. Their training and education focuses on business change and is designed to help deliver measurable outcomes related to the overall goals of the organization. Trailblazers develop and support a company-wide, strategic plan for inclusion and diversity that is broad based and comprehensive. *After* these goals are clear, the education and development programs are then designed—and delivered.

Once the company-wide strategy—including measurable outcomes—is completed, there are several steps that managers can take to make this training and education successful.

# Including Education and Training Measures in the Audit

Adding training and education outcomes as part of the overall inclusion and diversity accountability process allows you to measure your diversity training and education effectiveness, and then set goals to fine-tune the organization's actions to address the gaps. (A complete discussion of D & I accountability can be found in Chapter 5.)

Employees are rarely at "ground zero" in terms of their inclusion and diversity awareness. Without performing an audit to determine where you are versus where you want to be regarding results, your training and education efforts will be hit or miss. You'll waste time and money as you attempt to address your specific company culture's needs. On the other hand, an audit will elicit interest in and awareness of diversity issues and opportunities. The audit itself is a teaching tool, because responders learn through answering the questions. They also receive a positive message about management's vision and expectations.

An effective audit lies in the quality of its questions. You want to develop questions that focus on outcomes and desired behaviors that are based on the cultural competencies identified within your diversity plan. To aid the training development process, determine how the competencies will be addressed within the workshop sessions. Cross-reference each audit question/statement as it relates to a cultural competency.

Below are a few audit statement examples:

- Employees in my organization actively question behaviors that reinforce biases or prejudice in the workplace. (Cultural Competency: acknowledging and respecting differences and similarities in people.)
- My manager listens to ideas from everyone and encourages input individually and/or as a group. (Cultural Competency: demonstrating inclusion as a way to engage the full workforce.)
- Our employees demonstrate a belief that everyone has a contribution to make, regardless of culture, gender, race, sexual orientation, etc. (Competency: openness and willingness to understand how culture—and other differences/similarities—affects working behaviors and relationships.)

- Employees are included in the decision-making process when appropriate for their jobs. (Cultural Competency: understanding the impact of differences on actions and interactions.)

## One Size Does Not Fit All

There is no "ideal" length of time for diversity training and education sessions. The critical question to answer is: "What do you want these sessions to accomplish?" Our Trailblazers offer gatherings on many diversity topics, in many formats, and with varying lengths. Many organizations determine the program's length without regard to the objectives they wish to achieve, thus setting themselves and the initiative up for failure. Organizations frequently expect major behavior change but will only make time for a half-day of training programs. To avoid this pitfall, it's best to clarify expected outcomes first, and then determine the most appropriate format and length needed to achieve the expected outcomes. This may require the sessions to be delivered in several modules over time, instead of all at once.

## Develop Processes Your Leaders Will Use to Reinforce the Learning Immediately and Long Term

Engaging managers in long-term cultural change is an absolute key to success. Our Trailblazers have used several techniques with positive results, one of which is to create something some call Diversity Moments. This builds on the notion of Safety Moments that organizations use to keep the spotlight on the importance of safety. At the beginning of all team and staff meetings, time is allotted on the agenda for a volunteer to share a Diversity Moment "aha" experience. For example, the employee might tell others about how she makes a point to sit with someone she does not already know in the company cafeteria once a week. One successful reinforcement technique is to grant "Diversity Dollars" that could be redeemed in the company store to buy various types of merchandise. If this is not an option, items such as movie passes or low-cost gift certificates to restaurants or online stores work equally as well. Each time employees share a Diversity Moment at a meeting, they receive a Diversity Dollar.

## Develop an Effective Evaluation Process

Instead of basing your understanding of the workshops' success solely on one evaluation survey, use the Four Levels of Evaluation developed by Donald Kirkpatrick. The first level—often called the "smile sheet"—provides immediate reaction to the workshop and can help you determine if you are using the right facilitators, if the length is sufficient, if content was understood, and if the participants enjoyed the session.

Level 2 evaluation assesses transfer of learning through the use of pretests and posttests, or assessments. This tool should focus on the inclusion and diversity competencies upon which the training was developed.

Level 3 measures behavior change, which one can evaluate by observing managers and employees. As you develop inclusion and diversity competencies for the organization, include a subset of actions/behaviors that demonstrate each competency, and be sure to include training exercises that demonstrate these behaviors. Then design fun ways to recognize and reward the new behaviors as a way of measuring the transfer of learning to action. Below is an example.

---

**Inclusion and Diversity Competency: Values and Respects All People.**

- **Action:** Listen to and encourage input of diverse ideas from others. Conduct training intervention to reinforce this competency. Role-play a team discussion where the team leader proactively elicits input.

- **Recognition/Reward:** Host an annual awards program to honor employees and leaders who have demonstrated diversity and inclusion competencies. For example, a client company honored an employee for initiating a community diversity discussion forum that now meets quarterly.

Level 4 evaluation focuses on business results. Managers can track increased retention of diverse group members, promotions, improved innovation within teams, and other factors to determine if the changing company culture is impacting the bottom line. Our Trailblazers offer a variety of inclusion and diversity workshops with clear and specific focus. For example, a workshop on selling to the multicultural market has a final evaluation that can be measured by the increased number of new clients or customers from target markets, or the increased sales of products developed and sold to emerging markets.

## Identify the Facilitators for Delivery of Inclusion and Diversity Efforts

There are advantages and disadvantages to both internal and external trainers and facilitators. Internal facilitators know the company, its culture, and its politics; thus they can relate workshop activities directly to workplace realities. This helps participants transfer the inclusion and diversity concepts to real-world applications quickly. But the disadvantage of using internal facilitators is they often inadvertently display their own biases through tone of voice, body language, and side comments. While these behaviors are sometimes unintentional, they can be deliberate as well. To be effective, internal facilitators need to complete their own personal inclusion and diversity work *before* attempting to deliver a workshop on such topics. If the internal trainers are required to lead these sessions even if they are not interested, then they will clearly be ineffective.

Facilitating a diversity workshop is unlike leading any other kind of training workshop. Participant opinions in these cases are personal and connected to their core belief structures, so the facilitator's role is to create a safe, nonthreatening learning environment for people to discover issues for themselves. Leaders must resist the temptation to make judgment statements or share personal beliefs as though they are absolutes. For instance, although a facilitator may have strong beliefs about religion or sexuality, he or she must remember that their opinion is just that. They must not assume that their viewpoint is the only "right" one, and they must strive to remain neutral while allowing participants to explore their own beliefs.

In order for facilitators to sustain impartiality and develop personal diversity competencies, they must commit to continuously exploring their own values, biases, stereotypes, and core beliefs. If internal trainers are not dedicated to the company's intended outcomes for these sessions, they're likely to sabotage the program.

Using external facilitators to deliver these workshops helps to avoid the pitfalls and challenges that are inherent with internal facilitators. External leaders can overcome the challenge of lacking an institutional history with the company by engaging in team teaching opportunities or spending some time getting to know the organization. Some techniques for doing so include interviews, focus groups, a review of company information and communications, and so on. External facilitators provide an advantage with their ability to be detached from internal politics. Thus, they are able to guide others' learning without worrying about the impact on their own career. Additionally—and perhaps most importantly—they bring the experience and insights of working with several organizations to the workshop. Of course, to determine whether your training and workshops are having the effect you desire, it's necessary to measure the results.

## Evaluate All Company Training and Education from a Diversity Perspective

You'll want to conduct a yearly evaluation of all training and education to ascertain whether the programs are inclusive and support the company's diversity message. For example, do your customer service lessons address cultural and gender-based differences? Does your new hire orientation include an overview of disabled-accessible entrances and exits? Auditing training programs is another way to demonstrate that inclusion and diversity is integrated into *all* company efforts—instead of being part of a separate program.

## Develop Scorecards for Diversity and Inclusion Training

It's also vital to track and report key inclusion and diversity education results regularly as they relate to the goals you've set. Reporting the results of more than one evaluation process will allow you to identify and justify the time and money you're investing in these programs.

Just as a car's dashboard includes several key indicators for the vehicle's optimal functionality, a diversity and inclusion dashboard will show you how well your programs are doing. It should be developed for the organization's full diversity and inclusion strategy with indicators related to training and education. The training and development department can then develop its own method to track progress toward its departmental goals for this area. (See Chapter 5 for more detailed information about metrics, dashboards, and scorecards.)

## What Trailblazers Are Saying and Doing . . .

### IBM

Trailblazer Ron Glover describes his company's actions as Diversity 1.0, 2.0 and now Diversity 3.0™—in the following way:

> "IBM has a long history of commitment to diversity and has consistently taken the lead on these kind of policies. It began in the mid-twentieth century, grounded in Equal Opportunity legislation and compliance (Diversity 1.0). We moved forward to Diversity 2.0 in the 1990s with a focus on eliminating barriers and understanding regional constituencies and differences between the constituencies. As our demographics changed, we adapted our workplace to be more flexible and began our focus on work-life integration. In addition, over the past 5 years, we've introduced IBM's Values, which links to our diversity work.
>
> This strong foundation brings us to where we are today: Diversity 3.0. This is the point where we can take best advantage of our differences—for innovation. Our diversity is a competitive advantage, and consciously building diverse teams helps us drive the best results for our clients. People development is about enabling the capability of our employees, managers, and teams to drive business performance. It focuses on providing our workforce with the tools, resources, and guidance needed to broaden our

knowledge base and develop skills most valued by our industry. It also allows employees the opportunity for career progression."

This clear vision prompts IBM to offer diversity education at the global, managerial, and employee levels. Their programs address a broad spectrum of inclusion, both internally and in the marketplace.

Randy MacDonald, IBM senior vice president of Human Resources, sums up the commitment this way.

"Our workforce's expertise is as critical to our success as the effectiveness of our technology. We invest more than $750 million annually to help make sure that our employees have leading-edge skills and ongoing development opportunities."

## Andrews Kurth, LLP

Partner and CDO Elizabeth Campbell of corporate and litigation law firm Andrews Kurth, LLP, provides excellent examples of how to make diversity sessions come alive to make strong and memorable points: "In many respects, this generational piece (of diversity) could almost trump some of the others—because it goes across so many different areas." Campbell continues, "I'm doing quite a bit of research and study on the area right now, because I really see that as sort of the next frontier. Our firm has already started training and education on this; we've started with our partners. So I'm very proud of the firm and what we've done. But all of this is really appreciating difference.

"In some of my training and education sessions I use two films in particular. The first is *Apollo 13* (which I've used before; but now that I live in Houston it really is underscored). I use the scene 'We have a problem' to demonstrate teamwork, and I've used other scenes to show people—and in this case, people who are all Caucasian—who represent different competencies and are from different companies. They were from independent contractors, they worked for NASA, they had different functions, they had different responsibilities; and they were challenged."

"There are these various teams that have to pull together under extraordinary circumstances to save the lives of the astronauts. There is one scene in particular where the astronauts are reporting a problem with $CO_2$. They have more astronauts in the lunar module then they planned, so the ventilation system is not adequate; they have to change the filter. They call down to Houston and say, 'Our readings are such, and we're losing oxygen. We don't have enough fresh air.'

"Mission Control figures out that they have to change the filter; but the problem is they don't have the equipment up there to change it. So they pull together this disparate group of engineers and other people to come up with a solution to make this new filtering system work. The participants are given a whole box of items to work with that are replicas of the only equipment that is up there on the spacecraft.

"They dump out the box's contents, and are told to 'figure it out.' No task in the project plan tells them what they have to do, and they have to bring together their different backgrounds and expertise to solve the problem at hand. *That* is teamwork. The similarity here is that of mission and goal, but the difference is the job you're doing. You're an economist or mathematician, you're a communication specialist, you're a mechanical engineer, and all of you must sit down and figure it out. And they do."

"The other film I use is *Remember the Titans*, a great one to use on leadership and teamwork to show a racially charged environment where you're bringing two teams together, and there is friction at almost every single level. But they focus on commonality of mission and purpose, and they want to win. Then everyone realizes they can win as a team and they pull together. And some people get booted off the team, because they're not supporting the group as a whole."

"You might wonder what this has to do with diversity? Well, diversity is a change management strategy. You're often altering your approach of doing something, or going from a traditional method to leading through inclusion and diversity strategies. We have to be prepared that, under stress and change, it's going to take some work. You have to keep going through, persevere, and stay on point. But that is the strength of a leader: to keep the group on task even in change."

"Diversity recognizes that not everyone comes from the same background and has the same primary language. We need to accommodate that in order to be effective in our business goals.

"There is an episode of *I Love Lucy* called 'Paris At Last!' (Feb. 27, 1956) where Lucy, Ricky, Fred and Ethel are traveling in Europe. Somehow, Lucy gets mixed up and ends up with passing counterfeit money. She finds herself in jail in France, ranting and raving that people don't understand a word she is saying. So Ricky comes to the rescue, of course, speaking broken English and Spanish—and they're in France. So no one understands him either.

"But they figure it out. There is an intoxicated person in the cell next to Lucy who speaks French and German; and then there is some-one else who speaks German and Spanish; and Ricky can do Spanish and English; and Lucy is only English. So they come up with a chain and it's repeated so the orders are delivered in French and then com-municated all the way to Lucy, and then Lucy has a response and communicates it back. It works; it's creative; it's teamwork. It is about understanding differences and then working through it.

"I try to set up my training and education sessions so that people will enjoy the experience and not just look at their watch and say to themselves, 'Okay, how soon can we leave?' The sessions are only an hour, so I limit my expectations, themes, and objectives to material we can cover in an interactive way inside this time limit.

"We bring a lot of our own personal issues to these kinds of situ-ations, and then it can get out of control. There is a whole line of training and education that I've done which really talks about filters. It goes something like this: If you're predisposed to think something, then everything you hear and see will fall into that bucket. If I'm pre-disposed to see differences between you and me, then I'll react to everything you say by thinking, 'See, there is another difference, and there's another difference,' because that's all I'm seeing. Since I am predisposed that's what I immediately see.

"On the other hand, if I look at you and say, 'Oh there is so much we have in common'—then that is what I tend to focus on. It's really funny because it happens automatically; it's innate in people. I try to get my groups to first recognize the similarities. I just watch, and sometimes they can do this quickly, while sometimes they just see the differences—and it's harder to get the similarities."

## Dell

Dell's diversity strategy is focused on driving an environment of inclusion that embraces and accepts employees as an integral part of the team—wherever they work. According to Gil Casellas, CDO, "We are committed to cross-cultural training and education, and eliminating barriers that hinder our multicultural team from achieving their personal and professional best. Additionally, working successfully with people from different cultures and countries is a skill that greatly impacts Dell's ability to compete in the global markets we serve."

Casellas continues, "What we do around training and educating the managers at the next level is still in the works. We have basic annual global diversity training and education and related activities. We have policies in place regarding the need to have diverse candidate slates for hiring and promotions, review of performance, etc. So all that architecture is in place, and has been for a while.

"The next step for us is to figure out how to globalize these tactics. That is what we're working on right now. It's a work in progress: how to embed these kinds of changes and get people to think more broadly and less U.S.-specific."

## Citi

Ana Duarte-McCarthy, Chief Diversity Officer for Citi, states that, "We are starting to look specifically at the retention of women who go through some of our advancement leadership training and education programs to see what their mobility is. Are they being promoted? Do they have expanded responsibility? We're trying to analyze areas we think are short of these catalyst opportunities to better support advancement.

"I have not set up separate systems for women of color, but I'm making sure they are part of anything we do. For example, we are doing a lot now for women's leadership development by focusing very specifically on how women get leadership training and education at a particular level. We conduct a survey to ascertain who high potentials are; and we ensure that women are part of this distribution.

"However, we also ask: Where are the women of color? We want to understand what part this group plays in terms of high potential distribution. If we're going to have a particular training and education or development program, we want to ensure that women of color are part of that. So we're not setting up anything specifically separate because we want them to be part of the priority funding and resources. Then we do something if there are opportunities. For example, we hold a multicultural women's conference with a group called Working Mother."

## The Coca-Cola Company

"Our diversity education efforts have moved from minimizing differences to amplifying, respecting, and valuing them to help drive business results," says Steve Bucherati, Coca-Cola CDO. "We know that ongoing training helps drive employee engagement and create a work environment that visibly values and leverages diversity and accelerates productivity. Our required diversity training for associates provides an overview of related management strategies in the workplace, as well as ways to effectively implement them with an inclusive approach. We also offer supplier diversity training to help ensure that associates understand how to leverage the procurement power of the company by creating a pool of suppliers that include minority- and women-owned businesses."

Bucherati becomes animated in his speech when discussing the company's commitment to diversity and inclusion education. "The Coca-Cola Company offers four different types of classes, plus a diversity speakers' series. Each course has a specific focus that is stated in its title. They are called The Business Case for Diversity, Managing in a Diverse Environment, and Micro-Inequities. The fourth course called Challenge Day, is a highly experiential program that helps participants understand how bias and discrimination impact all groups of people." (For details, see www.challengeday.org.) Steve believes emphatically that diversity and inclusion efforts miss the boat if they do not also include fairness in the equation. The training and all other diversity and inclusion actions embrace this concept at The Coca-Cola Company.

---

### INCLUSION INSIGHTS

- Diversity and inclusion training *by itself* does *not* work. It's necessary to build the strategic plan *before* launching related training and education—which should then become an integral part of the larger plan.
- An ideal approach is to segment the training; don't try to include everything in one workshop.
- Separate programs that focus on EEO and Affirmative Action compliance from those that focus on leveraging

inclusion and diversity for improved workplace climate and team building.

- Carefully consider *who* delivers the educational sessions. There are pluses and minuses to support using internal and external facilitators.

- Keep it real. Develop interactive sessions that build awareness and focus on skill building to help participants understand the expectations regarding behavior—and how it supports the culture the organization is building and sustaining.

- Conduct an inclusion and diversity audit on all training programs to ensure the diversity message is visible and consistent across all education efforts.

- Create a D & I dashboard and scorecard that includes training to track progress toward goal achievement.

- Execute and evaluate results. Rely on evidence beyond the immediate post-training evaluations. Identify and measure learning transfer and behavior change. Then determine how best to include these results on the business scorecard along with other measures.

# 8

## Sticky Strategies™ to Keep Your Pipeline Filled

nticipating Kathryn Bigelow's historic 2010 Best Director Oscar win, Jodie Foster was quoted as saying, "Directing is the one area that hasn't changed dramatically at all in the film business for women. I don't think it's a conspiracy, I don't think it's a plot to keep women down. I think it's really like race psychology. It's very hard to hand someone $8 million who doesn't look like you."[1]

In this, the twenty-first century, there are no acceptable excuses for not having a diverse pipeline of talent! Yet businesses continue to struggle. Although there are challenges, Trailblazers have been innovative in their approaches to overcome them. "We just can't find any . . ." is not accepted by these thought leaders. Diversifying any organization requires an investment of finances and time along with a commitment to change organizational behaviors while creating a culture of inclusion. No small task, but certainly an achievable one.

As this book went to print, the United States and countries in many parts of the world are still suffering from the effects of a major economic downturn, yet our Trailblazers are steadfast in their efforts to continue to attract and retain the best talent. Though never complacent, they realize that this is the time to work even harder than usual to retain and attract new talent. On March 9, 2010, *DiversityInc Magazine* announced its prestigious list of Top 50 Companies for Diversity. Trailblazer Sodexo is number one. Although representation is only one area of measurement, at Sodexo American Indians, Asians, African Americans, and Latinos are 50 percent of their workforce and 20 percent of senior management. During our interview with Sodexo's Rohini Anand, Senior Vice President and Global Diversity Officer, she explained the foundation for their success: "Our global strategy is built around talent excellence, operational excellence, and business excellence. It is built around clear goals that have to do with diversity in the pipeline, which includes recruiting, retaining, and engaging diverse populations. Across the globe we've focused on gender because it is the one thing that you can put metrics around. But it is more than just getting the bodies in those positions. Rather, we need to cast the net wide and hire the best qualified candidates, making sure we're changing behaviors and cultures in the organization."

## Finding the Right First Step

Once organizations decide to proactively foster a diverse culture, they almost immediately turn to the topic of recruitment of people from underrepresented groups. This tactic is comparatively easy and quick if processes are already in place to aggressively recruit underrepresented groups, and relatively easy to measure, so obtaining leadership buy-in and financial support for what in reality is woman and minority recruitment, but is often called "diversity" recruitment is relatively painless. Yet, this is a big mistake! We have constantly heard businesses complain that they wasted time and money because women and minorities just won't stay with their company. Our research (see Chapter 12), as well as that of others, repeatedly bears out the fact that the organizational culture must first be prepared for new faces, new perspectives, and new ways of achieving results before the onboarding of people from groups who have been underrepresented in the past. This does not mean all minority recruiting efforts should be halted until the culture changes. It does mean efforts should already be in place to create an inclusive culture free of bias and open to different perspectives. Efforts that create an environment to support and respect diversity in its broadest sense need to be in place if diversity recruiting is to be successful. This is a journey, not a destination. Both elements—recruiting and cultural change—are needed, not an "either–or."

An ever-popular training video, "A Peacock in the Land of Penguins,"[2] illustrates this dilemma beautifully. The penguin leaders decide a little diversity would be good for the company so they hire a peacock. Perry the Peacock is thrilled and thinks he can climb the corporate ladder simply by being good at his job. The video then illustrates how the penguins try to change Perry into a penguin-like peacock. Perry and his other colleagues of difference eventually give up and/or leave the organization because they are not accepted for who they are and the different perspectives they bring. Just like in the real world. The video demonstrates what happens when an organization hires underrepresented people without preparing the culture to effectively utilize diverse talent and create an environment of inclusion simultaneously.

# Sticky Strategies™ That Work

For pipeline development to be successful, many components are needed.

- Sourcing and recruiting
- Orientation and onboarding
- Mentoring, sponsoring, and coaching
- Succession planning
- Representation tracking
- Assignment reviews
- Employee survey and cultural audits

All are needed in conjunction with each other for the system to produce positive results.

## Sourcing and Recruiting: Finding the Talent

According to a recent global study that included executive respondents from 47 countries and conducted by the Society of Human Resource Management (SHRM), 53 percent of the respondents said tapping into a broader range of skills was the rationale for their diversity initiatives, and 43 percent indicated their rationale was based on the need for talent that understands their diverse customers in order to increase sales.[3]

Sourcing requires careful planning and execution at each step. Let's explore the elements of Sticky Strategies™.

### Define Success

Determine what demographics you wish to target and what skill sets and competencies your organization needs now and in the future. Having a laser approach versus a scattered one will provide higher levels of success. Does your organization want to attract more talented women? People of color? Veterans? People with disabilities? Where is the focus?

Francene Young, VP of Talent and Diversity at Shell, described it this way: "The 'D' part of diversity is to find the smartest, most innovative people in a commodity business that can help us move forward. So, in addition to recruiting at the top ten universities, we seek out women who we haven't sought out before, as well as African Americans. That strategy leads us to actively recruit at HBCUs (Historically Black Colleges and Universities). Once we get them in place, we really push the 'I', which is the inclusion, to ensure that people are contributing to the very best of their ability without the blockers."

We are not suggesting that people should be hired because of their differences. Skill and performance are essential, and are therefore table stakes. Rather, candidates who have a different perspective and point of view due to their difference of culture, ethnicity, gender, and so forth. should be valued as an asset. Research shows that the best innovation and problem solving occur when teams are (1) most diverse; there is (2) common issue to be resolved; and (3) there is a strong respect for the individual differences that each person brings, that is, when there is diversity. Thus, hiring the best talent includes making sure a company's pool of talent reflects diversity and supports inclusion. (For a more detailed discussion of this point, read *The Medici Effect*, by Frans Johansson.)

### Assess Current Activities and Their Results

Review your sourcing efforts for general recruiting. What works well? What general sources could be tapped for targeted recruiting? With the tight focus on expenses, look to collaborate and combine efforts. For example, when you advertise in "mainstream" magazines for your organization, broaden your reach by designing ads that speak to the visual dimensions of inclusion and diversity. If you are already using executive search firms to source talent, you might redirect some of your efforts and dollars by using minority and women owned business enterprises (MWBE) that specialize in multicultural recruiting. Additionally, advise your mainstream advertising firms of your expectations that they utilize MWBEs in their second tier sourcing and that they outsource to minority and women owned firms to assist them with a deeper reach into a particular market segment.

### Identify What You Will Need to Do Differently to Reach Diverse Talent

Being successful at multicultural recruiting takes time, persistence, and patience. Just posting job descriptions on multicultural job boards on the Internet or placing a few ads in targeted magazines is not enough. Multicultural candidates from entry level to executive are looking for organizations that show an interest in their communities and respect for their perspectives. Partner with your employee resource groups (ERGs) to develop tactics to reach new markets (see Chapter 14). ERGs will help you avoid making costly mistakes and will help you identify unique ways to develop and sustain and authentic presence.

An automotive client (not a Trailblazer company) wanted to reach out to the women's market in order to develop a presence and ultimately attract female mid-level managers to join their organization. The company identified a nationally recognized women's business organization and developed a plan to partner with them by holding clinics at their dealerships to teach women how to buy a car. After involving their Women's ERG, the company totally revamped their plan. What they learned through the Women's ERG is that the original plan the company intended to use was flawed and perceived as condescending. The Women's ERG had connected directly with women business owners who purchased and leased fleets of cars and trucks and were responsible for millions of dollars. Through their conversations with them, they learned that the original approach would not achieve the results they sought. Had the original program been launched, it would have significantly damaged the company's reputation in the marketplace, instead of enhancing it among the very businesswomen they were targeting. To conclude this story, the Women's ERG then partnered with the marketing team to create a more inclusive and very effective approach.

### Use Social Media Strategies to Reinforce Your Diversity Brand and Surface Talent

The world of social networking is growing and changing as fast as the shape of an amoeba. Today's best social networking site is tomorrow's has-been. The exponential growth will continue for several years, but that should not be a reason to avoid playing in this arena. One of the best ways to source talent is through word of mouth, that is, referrals. Use social media strategically to further your reach and your message.

### Make Sure Diversity Recruiting Messages Are Congruent with the Company Brand

Your diversity recruiting initiatives should be a complement to other sourcing and recruiting activities as well as to the overall efforts the business makes to build brand eminence. If these initiatives are sporadic or disjointed, your results will reflect the same.

### Use a Combination of Targeted and General Marketing to Obtain Holistic Results

Allstate illustrates this well. They selected Dennis Haysbert, an African American actor from the popular action-drama TV show *The Unit*, to be their spokesperson. Choosing a Black man to be *the* company spokesman is a first in an industry regarded by many as very conservative. Using Haysbert was a smart marketing move for several reasons. The ad is a general commercial regarding the benefits of selecting Allstate as an insurance company. The ad is not a recruitment advertisement. Because Haysbert is known to the general public due to his role in *The Unit*, and he is known by most African American women over the age of 25 due to the role he played along with Whitney Houston in the movie *Waiting to Exhale*, he "speaks volumes" for the company's attitude about inclusion without ever mentioning the word. This presence helps tip the scales when multicultural candidates consider Allstate for employment, and multicultural consumers in particular consider Allstate for their insurance company.

### Expect Diverse Talent in Every Pool of Candidates

The only way to increase representation of diverse talent within the organization is to increase the pool of candidates from which you select. Companies do themselves and the candidates a disservice when only one minority or woman candidate is included in the interview pool. For every job level where more diversity is needed, we suggest having at least three diverse candidates among the entire pool of candidates. This helps interviewing managers evaluate all candidates based on the skills and abilities they offer without having one individual represent a whole group. When there is only one person of difference available, their difference tends to stand out more than their talents. Imagine a bowl of red delicious apples. Now imagine the same bowl with one green apple. The green apple may have many attributes, but the only thing the eye will see is its color. Add a few more green apples and no one apple stands out alone.

### *Multicultural Candidates Look for Long-Term Diversity and Inclusion Commitment*

Your committed support of national and local organizations that serve diverse populations does not go unnoticed by job candidates. Your community support is an indicator of your support of diversity and inclusion within the company (see Chapter 9). Trailblazer IBM's Corporate Service Corps is similar to a corporate version of the Peace Corps. It sends teams of eight to ten top performing employees from around the world, with skills in technology, consulting, research, marketing, and finance, to key emerging markets for one month. This program provides quadruple benefits: (1) an opportunity of a lifetime for the employee; (2) unique leadership development for IBM's talent pipeline; (3) communities receive hundreds of thousands of dollars worth of free expert consulting services and advice; and (4) the global community involvement projects send positive messages about IBM's commitment to diversity. This combination—sticky strategy—positively impacts recruitment, retention, and advancement. Prepare recruiters and interviewing managers by providing diversity and inclusion education that includes a recruiting and onboarding component.

Once you create the circumstances that attract the best talent, make sure your company representatives are ready to take it to the next level. This team needs to be well-versed in all the diversity and inclusion efforts of the company. They should be able to speak to the company's commitment to diversity and inclusion as they conduct behavioral interviews and look for the candidate's ability to model D & I competencies during the interview.

## Orientation and Onboarding

As we are using it here, onboarding includes all of the steps an organization uses immediately following the job offer, including orientation to help the new employee assimilate into the culture of the organization more seamlessly; therefore orientation includes all of the steps used to bring the employee up to speed after hire. Many organizations call the entire combined process onboarding. Trailblazers use a variety of Sticky Strategies™ in their orientation and onboarding efforts to drive a culture of inclusion: face-to-face meetings, eLearning programs, ongoing webinars, the buddy system, and the employee handbook are formats sometimes used. Half of the Trailblazers use all of the above to effectively communicate expectations, company values, and culture. In addition, ongoing awareness and appreciating diversity courses, intranet employee communications, diversity speaker series, and consistent and continuous leadership messages all contribute to sustaining the message of inclusion.

Our research (Chapter 12) indicated a strong correlation between the early experiences of diverse employees and their willingness to stay with the company. This is generally true for all employees, but it is particularly important for talent that is different than the majority. The first 90 days are important as the new employee is further assessing the environment of the workplace, how comfortable they will be in it, while all the time delivering on the contributions they are expected to make.

As you assess your company's onboarding and orientation process, ask the following questions:

1. Where are the touch points in the onboarding process timetable that speak to the company's values regarding diversity and inclusion? Are they articulated up front or are they buried within the process?
2. What are executives saying—and when—about diversity and inclusion?
3. Are seasoned employees proactive in their efforts to help the new employees feel included? How are they accomplishing this?
4. On average, how soon do new employees become productive?
5. Among women and minorities who leave the company, at what point in their tenure does this tend to happen most often (e.g.,

90 days, two years, five years)? What is or is not happening at those critical points? What do your exit interviews tell you?

6. How often do you want an employee to receive performance feedback during the first year? How is this communicated?

7. Are managers capable of providing effective feedback to all employees, but especially to women and people of color? What barriers need to be eliminated in order for this to happen?

8. Are women and people of color being mentored to the same degree as their White male counterparts? How big of an issue is this?

## Mentoring, Sponsoring, and Coaching

*"When we look for differences, we find them. When we seek similarities, we find those too. The wise person searches for both, and in so doing discovers an individual."*

—Fran Rees

We believe the wise leader seeks to understand both differences and similarities within emerging leaders and then chooses to guide and mentor others.

On the other hand, look what happens when opportunities are overlooked. Take the case of Donald.[4] Donald was hired as an electrical technician by a utility company. The company leadership was proud of its accomplishment because Donald was highly skilled and deaf. They felt they were being both progressive and inclusive. However, after being onboard for about five years, Donald shared with us that he was still in the exact same job, and he was rarely included in professional development training and education programs because the company had to pay for Sign Language interpreters for the full length of the program if he attended. He received mandatory technical training in order to keep up with changes impacting his certifications and specific duties. Donald said that although his pay increases were adequate, no one had ever asked him what his career aspirations were. After five years, no manager had attempted to learn more about him and his aspirations. When Donald brought up the subject, it seemed to him as if no one thought it important enough to engage him in more than a cursory conversation without much depth, and for no more than a few minutes. He believed the company dropped any responsibility for his professional development because of his disability. Whether his perception was factual or not, it was his reality.

How might Donald have benefited by having a mentor? Could this oversight have been avoided if he had had a sponsor who knew his work and could help him understand how to approach these conversations more effectively?

The practice of mentoring, sponsoring, and coaching have been around for a very long time. There are many definitions and descriptions for all three leadership development tactics. For the sake of this conversation we are using the following definitions:

*Mentoring*—a developmental sharing, caring, and helping relationship where an experienced leader (mentor) invests time with an emerging leader (mentee or protégé) in order to enhance the growth, knowledge, and skills of the emerging leader. The mentor provides guidance and enlightened advice regarding the unwritten rules of success. Mentors are usually, but not required to be, employees of the organization. Some people also have mentors within a profession. The use of the word *leader* in this case does not imply that mentoring only happens with management-level employees. It occurs at all levels. A mentor relationship might last years, or, if it is part of a formal program, it may last six months to a year.

*Coaching*—a coach is one who helps others expand their thinking, usually with the focus on exploring possibilities to enhance their ability to achieve future results. Today, many executives utilize the services of an executive coach in order to help them clarify their strengths, and become more effective leaders. The length of coaching engagements may vary from several months to a year. Individuals are typically coached (1) to enhance their leadership effectiveness, (2) for positioning for another assignment of greater responsibility, and (3) for performance.

*Sponsoring*—sponsors are individuals who create or support opportunities of advancement and growth for emerging leaders. The emerging leader may or may not know s/he has a sponsor. These are often people who observe from a distance and open doors of opportunity through dialogue, especially during closed door sessions when an individual's performance is being assessed.

A study conducted by Columbia Business School and the executive search firm Korn/Ferry found that 80 percent of high-level minority executives lack formal mentors and nearly 33 percent don't have informal mentors.[5] All of our Trailblazers have had mentors and/or coaches and many still do. All of our Trailblazers are mentors to others within and outside their organizations. Research conducted by Catalyst[6] and others, including our findings, repeatedly indicate women and other minorities in the workplace are better able to succeed within their organization if they have a mentor. Mentors often bridge the gap of initial informal networking opportunities with higher level executives.

As consultants, we have experienced a rapidly increasing demand for coaching over the past five to ten years. Coaching is 100 percent focused on helping a manager or leader improve some critical aspect of their performance or professional development. Rarely is coaching used to address major problems. For this, other means are used.

Diversity-related mentor programs can be informal or formal. The majority of our Trailblazers have a formal mentoring process within their company and they provide training for the mentor and the mentee. There are advantages to both the formal and the informal process. A formal process helps avoid overlooking an emerging leader's need for or interest in having a mentor. It makes it easier to administer mentoring training on a scheduled basis. It is easier to measure the results of the pairing. And its training can address special issues such as the challenges of cross-gender mentoring. Informal mentoring avoids the problem of mismatched pairs. It often lasts longer, but it is sometimes harder to measure the results.

Many Trailblazers hold their executives accountable by requiring that they serve in the role of mentor to one or more emerging leaders. In some cases, their compensation, usually bonuses, is tied to their participation as a mentor.

Additionally, mentoring occurs through employee resource groups and outside organizations that specialize in developing minority and women leaders. For over 50 percent of our Trailblazers, the Vice President of Human Resources administers the mentoring program, and for others the responsibility resides with the CDO. The Vice President of Organizational Effectiveness or Learning also holds responsibility for formal mentoring programs with many organizations.

There are excellent models for mentoring programs. To ensure the highest level of success for your efforts, include the following components:

- Assess pipeline needs to ensure your efforts include underrepresented groups.
- Develop a process that works best for your environment.
- Educate both the mentor and the mentee to set expectations, goals, and timelines to ensure the effectiveness of the relationship.
- Utilize both formal and informal mentoring.
- Hold leaders accountable for the results through the performance management system.
- Measure success.
- Reward positive results.

## Succession Planning

Succession planning goes hand-in-hand, and beyond mentoring programs. As you determine who has potential for leadership, incorporating a mentoring component into that person's development plan is a common practice for forward-thinking companies. As you observed in Figure 3.1, the CDO plays an integral role in making sure all of the diversity initiatives are focused on the overall objectives of the organization. Nowhere is this more evident than in the succession planning process. The primary business case for most organizations' efforts in diversity and inclusion is to attract and retain the best talent to meet their business needs. Making sure that "top talent" is identified, developed, and included in the succession planning process is critical. An overwhelming majority of our Trailblazers are involved in the identification and discussions about the success and development of all individuals, inclusive of those who are women and people of color.

## Representation Tracking

*"You are accountable to establish the right expectations. Those expectations must be driven by your values and challenge you to grow. The best expectations are based not only on your historical data but also on the experiences of others."*
—Sam Silverstein, Author of *No More Excuses*

As previously noted in the beginning of the diversity movement, education was the first thing most companies provided, followed by or simultaneously with representation tracking. In the twenty-first century, representation tracking and an inclusive culture have assumed an importance beyond a requirement. Organizations understand the cost of onboarding, developing, and retaining the best talent for today's competitive global marketplace. Thus, keeping track of what is happening with that talent pool is critical to the organization's ability to improve in this regard. As Silverstein says in the above quote, your responsibility as a leader includes shaping expectations—in this case, shaping expectations of others as it relates to the company's reasons for tracking talent. CDOs can help leaders articulate these expectations in a way that effectively expresses the business reasons to do so.

Trailblazers monitor many factors as it relates to the diversity and inclusion efforts of their businesses. They track a wide variety of representation categories and take action when their dashboards indicate a potential problem. The representation categories most often tracked and compared are:

- Women overall
- Women by racial group
- Men overall
- Men by racial group
- Generational age categories overall
- Generational age—women overall
- Generational age—women by racial group
- Generational age—men by racial group

For Trailblazers, these numbers provide the basis for determining effective recruiting, professional development, succession planning, and mentoring initiatives. Effective CDOs monitor and measure results to support the business case for diversity and inclusion by helping others see the opportunities gained and missed when diversity and inclusion initiatives are not a core part of the human resources strategies and processes.

Effective pipeline development requires all stakeholders to understand their role in success. The most effective leaders recognize they must create and sustain an environment that is inclusive and reflects their communities, clients, and customers if they intend to make their organization "sticky" and enhance their business growth by attracting and retaining the best talent on the globe.

---

### INCLUSION INSIGHTS

- Make sure your D & I pipeline commitment, accomplishments, awards, and other relevant information are very visible and easy to access on your web site. The standard is no more than two clicks away from the home page.
- Review all aspects of your onboarding process to ensure it reflects the culture of inclusion the organization desires.
- Carefully consider and initiate a mentoring program to enhance leadership development. Hold leaders accountable for advancing all their people through the performance management process. Encourage reverse mentoring.
- Top performing companies include the CDO for his or her insights in the succession planning process.
- Monitor representation of women, people of color, and by generation, to pinpoint areas of intervention for improving retention of the best talent.

# 9

# Community Involvement and Social Responsibility

## *Is It Just Good Public Relations or Is There More?*

## Community Involvement: A Responsibility and Good Business

There are many and varied definitions of community that can be accurately applied to business. Our primary focus, however, is on the relationship that organizations have with external communities or societies with whom they conduct business and/or geographies within which they are physically located. Our Trailblazers deem this relationship critical to the success of diversity and inclusion within their businesses, as this involvement drives results in several ways.

Although progressive leaders see community involvement as a corporate responsibility, none consider these actions to be "obligations" in the negative sense. Being responsible to the citizens you employ and serve is good business. Making sure these efforts relate to and support company diversity and inclusion credos and missions strengthens the business and defines the company's footprint in the marketplace.

**133**

Companies have known for years that supporting community efforts can reflect positively on the organization. So are these efforts just good public relations, or is there more? According to Citi CDO Ana Duarte-McCarthy, "We're seeing a correlation between corporate responsibility and community involvement, and people getting more engaged. Being involved with the community leads to having a better representation of employees that reflect the community." When employees believe that their organizations care about the communities in which they live, they are in turn more committed to the organization and more likely to be ambassadors for the company as they interact with their friends, family, and colleagues.

Sodexo CDO Rohini Anand summed this up well: "We were very, very focused internally and then realized at some point that the external community that we hadn't touched and hadn't engaged was out there. This is a community from which we recruit and in which we do business. So we needed to engage it by starting to build those community and external partnerships. I would say the tipping point came about four years into our journey. We had done all these things, and really invested it well. Our managers started seeing the business benefits of what we were doing in the external community."

## Linking Diversity Efforts and Community Involvement

Where, then, is the link between corporate diversity and community efforts? Trailblazers see many. According to Steve Bucherati, CDO at The Coca-Cola Company, community involvement is an integral component of strengthening the brand. He explains, "Our brands are for everyone; it doesn't matter whether you're the President of the United States or the average Jane or Joe on the street. You can't buy 'better' Coke, no matter how rich or who you are. The brand is truly inclusive. So we extrapolate from that and say, well, that's what we ought to be about as an organization. We ought to be as inclusive as our brands. We ought to be a company for everybody, no matter who you are, what your background is, and what your experiences are. Then we take that mentality and try to drive that down into our marketplace, workplace, and community strategies."

Michael Collins of American Airlines expresses it this way: "At our company, diversity and inclusion are not areas that we consider to be separate from what we're trying to accomplish in satisfying our customers, engaging our employees, participating in the community, and being a good corporate citizen. We talk about diversity as a continuum rather than an ending destination. It is something for which everyone is responsible, especially our leaders. In order to be a good leader, you need to be able to lead diversity and create inclusive environments."

Some businesses have very specific community goals, while others support community projects as they surface because they generally see it as the "right thing to do." Trailblazers help their organizations develop and clarify community involvement goals, and then they guide their leaders as they support the community agencies and projects that are in alignment with the company's mission and values. Instead of using the scattered, "here today, gone tomorrow" approach, Trailblazers help their companies focus their efforts and resources, often working with their Corporate Affairs and Community Involvement departments—which creates the ability to measure outcomes and make adjustments where needed. The more the company can focus its community involvement and professional association efforts, the more tangible their results will be.

Figure 9.1 illustrates the critical components of an effective community involvement process. First, the company must become clear

Leadership and
Employee Engagement

Brand and
Marketplace Clarity

Community
Involvement
and Philanthropy

ERG/CDO
Community Relations
Goal-setting

**FIGURE 9.1**  Community Involvement

about their brand and their marketplace. This then allows collaboration between the CDO, ERG leaders, and corporate responsibility/community relations departments in the goal-setting process. Once goals are set, communication, recognition, and rewards for involvement can be disseminated throughout the organization.

For example, Dell contributes significant time and dollars in the communities where their employees live and work by developing community programs that promote digital inclusion and close the gap on the digital divide. "We are committed to the belief that people around the world should have access to technology to learn critical skills and enhance their lives," says CDO Gil Casellas. Similarly, having built a global business on improving the effectiveness of written communication, Pitney Bowes has a vital interest in literacy and education. Their leadership believes that, by supporting literacy and education programs, the company can improve countless lives and strengthen the fabric of communities everywhere they are involved. Note that nowhere in these focus statements is there a mention of diversity and inclusion. There is no need. These are overall business statements where diversity and inclusion is implicit.

## Leading the Way through Supporting Professional Associations

Business executives serve on community boards of all types and for a variety of reasons; the following are just a few.

1. To advance the work of the community organization by publicly lending their name, time, and efforts as a board member.
2. To share their business knowledge with community organizations with which they have a personal interest, in order to help them grow.
3. To develop relationships that lead to positive business opportunities and/or identify potential future talent for the organization.
4. To develop knowledge and understanding of the needs of groups of people different from themselves.

When an organization has clear diversity and inclusion goals related to community involvement, its leaders' and employees' actions as community volunteers are more likely to elicit tangible results. When people know *why* they are serving their community—beyond it simply being the "right thing to do"—they're able to increase their awareness of how they might address specific community challenges. A few of our Trailblazer companies require their senior executives to serve the community in the capacity of volunteers and or board members, and this accountability is reflected in their salaries and bonuses. This deeper understanding of all of the people who make up the community allows executives to make more informed decisions regarding how their business impacts the community—and even their personal lives.

Steve Bucherati developed this deeper understanding over time and explains that it has impacted his career in a profound way. He says, "My background has been a collection of personal experiences that have allowed me—especially as a White male—to be involved in a number of community-based, personal, and organizational work that has gotten me very, very involved in what I'll call 'in and around' the diversity and inclusion space—but never in a direct way. Then when I came into the role as CDO, all of a sudden there was that recognition that all these life experiences were now coming full circle and giving me the opportunity to move things forward. I feel like it all worked out as almost a grand design. I love this work, and if I have it my way, I won't leave it."

> *"Human progress is neither automatic nor inevitable. . . . (It requires) the tireless exertions and passionate concern of dedicated individuals."*
> —Rev. Dr. Martin Luther King, Jr.

Executives of Trailblazer companies see the payoff that comes with supporting the external community and are clear about the inclusive connection. American Airlines' Mike Collins declares, "Because we serve people all over the world, it is imperative that we not only understand differences but also ensure our constituents know that we're aware of their needs. In the words of our Chairman and CEO, Gerard Arpey: 'As a company that bears the name "American," much is expected of us; and we hold ourselves to a high standard.' Our brand is directly connected to the diversity of our stakeholders." Kiersten Robinson, CDO of Ford, explains, "Our corporate reputation has been enhanced as a long-time supporter of diversity and the role we play—not only in the communities where we operate, but also the broader global community. It reaffirms Ford's strong commitment to a better world—a sustainability strategy, not just climate change, fuel economy, mobility, vehicle safety, but also in human rights to support positive social change."

## Building Bridges through Learning and Trust

Effective leaders discover they must first travel their own diversity journey before they can develop anything beyond a superficial understanding of people different from themselves. While it's easy to donate money, that is just a part of the role of corporate philanthropy. It's needed, but it doesn't allow for much engagement with the community on a personal level, and donations can be perceived as an attempt to garner good public relations instead of true commitment. Diversity and inclusion at all levels works when those involved develop trust; to do so, direct engagement must occur. It's tough to dedicate your personal time and build the courage of conviction— whether you're a busy executive or entry-level employee—until you have exposure to others on a personal level.

Progressive leaders are willing to be a little vulnerable in order to understand that perspectives different from their own are not wrong— just different. Most leaders are accustomed to having people see things their way. By personally supporting community organizations that serve diverse constituents, executives are able to broaden their perspectives.

There are countless programs across the country that focus on exposing executives to the potential of people within underrepresented groups. The national organizations that sponsor these programs have various mission statements, but they all share in a single goal: to open more doors of opportunity for disenfranchised or underrepresented individuals. These programs give leaders fresh perspectives while allowing them to discover great new talent. When leaders become involved at the grassroots and local level, they are more apt to see people in underrepresented groups as individuals, rather than clustering them together as a group. Although there are far too many organizations to mention here, our Trailblazers cite several long standing organizations that they routinely support at the national and/or local level.

- The Executive Council (www.execcouncil.org)
- The National Urban League (www.nul.org)

- Catalyst (www.catalyst.org)
- National Black MBA Association (www.nbmbaa.org)
- National Society of Hispanic MBAs (www.nshmba.org)
- National Diversity Council (www.nationaldiversitycouncil.org)
- Families and Work Institute (www.familiesandwork.org)
- Human Rights Campaign (www.hrc.org)
- Habitat for Humanity (www.habitat.org)
- National Organization on Disabilities (www.nod.org)
- Ascend for Pan Asian Leaders (www.ascendleadership.org)

The partnerships with these organizations are successful because:

1. Relationships work well when expectations are clearly defined and there is alignment in mission and approach with the organization.
2. Employee participation links to diversity and inclusion objectives.
3. They provide access to other underrepresented professionals as well as potential talent and other resources.
4. There is a strong collaboration and partnership with constantly evolving practices.
5. Those involved participate in making a tangible, positive difference in the lives of others.

Many locals support organizations that focus on community issues where diversity and inclusion intersect. One such program that has been highly successful is Impact Greensboro in North Carolina (www.impactgreensboro.org). The goal of this initiative is to create a vibrant networked community of "Change Agents" who are equipped to identify and tackle community issues. The organizers—Community Foundation of Greater Greensboro, University of North Carolina, Greensboro's Center for Youth, Family and Community Partnerships, and the City of Greensboro's Human Relations Department—recruit current and emerging leaders from all backgrounds, ages, and walks of life. The selected 50 participants engage in a yearlong dialogue about topics such as socioeconomics and homelessness, race, education, safety in neighborhoods, and other topics of community interest, while they learn how to be effective change agents. Leaders emerge at the end of the year with a deep understanding of the impact their decisions have on the broader community. When they're making choices that will influence an entire neighborhood or a specific group of people—who often don't have a voice at the decision-making table—they are better informed of the importance of seeking additional information from community stakeholders before making the decision.

We highlight this program and others like it such as Leadership America as examples of what people can do to create and support cohesive, future-focused communities. When leaders recognize the impact of their decisions regarding, for example, where to build a plant, what happens in workers' lives when one is closed, how utilizing diverse suppliers strengthens a city, or why sponsoring a specific educational program in secondary schools such as Junior Achievement they become better corporate citizens. These partnerships and shared learnings go far beyond just good public relations. It strengthens the notion that diversity and inclusion make the businesses more successful in the longer term.

*"Ubuntu—I am because we are. We are because I am."*
                                              —Zulu Proverb

# Engaging Employees for Increased Commitment

Trailblazers encourage and reward employees for their community involvement. When employees know their company supports the efforts in which they have a personal interest, they feel more connected to their employers. Employees who have the capacity to volunteer in their community become more informed citizens. They are better equipped to have a voice on social, socioeconomic, educational, and environmental issues when they know their company supports their time and efforts in the community. This involvement does more than provide a company presence in the community, and it goes beyond corporate responsibility. It also provides leadership development and diversity and inclusion awareness education to those involved. Employee community interests coupled with organizational diversity objectives related to the community create a win-win situation for all involved.

Before co-author Lenora Billings-Harris became a diversity strategist, she was a director of human resource management for a division of a Fortune 500 company. She and her husband are child-free by choice, and she decided to become a Big Sister in the local Big Brother Big Sister program while in that HR role. As often happens when volunteers first become involved with a community organization, she thought she would have much to give. However, she had barely considered how much she would receive by being involved with one teen-aged girl.

After two years of being a Big Sister to Charlotte, Lenora recognized how much her own life had been changed, how her perspective about teenagers, people of different socioeconomic backgrounds, single moms, and privilege had broadened. She knows all of these insights helped her become a better and more diversity-sensitive leader. At the same time, the company for which she worked built upon its positive reputation within the community because of the many efforts of leaders like her. These gratifying rewards abound among individuals and organizations that connect with their communities.

## Connecting to Global Communities

Our Trailblazers have found that becoming involved in global communities while supporting company goals is rewarding for employees, leaders, *and* the communities they impact. More often than not, "community" includes groups of people within certain geographies, as well as groups with common characteristics. Deb Dagit of Merck & Company shared the following example of how community and employee teams are able to innovate:

"We have a CEO diversity and inclusion award that we give on a global basis. It has given us a platform for employees at all levels of the organization not only to be recognized for individual efforts but team efforts as well, while articulating the business outcome.

"One of the teams that received recognition was the one that put together the approach to getting Gardasil (also known as Silgard, a vaccine to prevent certain types of human papillomavirus [HPV]) into the marketplace. They went about gathering voices of the customer, and designing the campaign called 'One Less.' We actually had people of all ages singing the little jingle and explaining what 'One Less' meant. The approach was very multicultural and respectful of different faiths, generations, and the role that mothers play in health care decisions. It was also respectful of young women themselves.

"That team went out into the communities, and really did a great job of understanding the community/marketplace. They designed an extraordinarily effective campaign that led to remarkable uptake of the product and, at the same time, demonstrated in very subtle ways how you can do this in a way that is multiculturally sensitive."

---

### INCLUSION INSIGHTS

1. Set clear and specific goals for community involvement, and communicate those goals to employees and leaders. Company leaders, ERGs, and CDOs must work in concert with the community relations department.

2. Support volunteerism and create mechanisms for employees to communicate the good work they are doing internally and externally. Give them credit for their work through the performance management system.

3. Conduct focus groups and connect community involvement to product development by finding ways to hear and include the voices of the people of the community on new products and services before launched.

4. Volunteer to learn as well as to advise. Participate in community projects and programs that will broaden your understanding of various groups of people who are different from you. Share your learnings with others.

5. Learn the mission and goals of key national and local professional organizations that align to your business objectives and partner with them regarding community talent management and community relations.

# 10

# Global Diversity and Inclusion

*"If you have not created an inclusive meritocracy in your home country, I don't know how you have the skills to go and do that with people in a different country whom you only talk with primarily by phone and deal with mostly by conference calls and emails. I just don't know how that's possible."*
—Ron Glover, Vice President of Diversity and Work Force Programs for the IBM Corporation

## Adopting a Global Mindset

The conversation around global diversity is not a new one; in fact, it's been going on for well over 15 years. What *is* different is the level of awareness and appreciation that Fortune 100, 500, and 1,000 organizations have obtained regarding inclusion and global diversity today versus what it was more than a decade ago. This knowledge is based in part upon the realities that the recent recession has forced into the conversation. People collectively understand better how highly interconnected—environmentally, humanitarily, and economically—we truly are. Our understanding now is greater, perhaps more so, than it was before the 2007 time frame when more and more countries were coming to grips with the dire effects of both the recession and devastating natural disasters. This increased comprehension of our global economies' interdependencies has underscored this truth at a very fundamental level; a truth that most of today's high school students recognize with crystal clarity by way of their economics courses and volunteerism experiences.

## Technology and Global Diversity

The advent of technology—and the ubiquitous influence of the Internet on our ability to acquire information and transact business in seconds for that which used to take weeks or days—has further elevated the conversation around global diversity. People today have at their disposal some of the most sophisticated processing systems and in-depth information-gathering tools available. They can learn about an organization, its culture and goals, and its viewpoint on the community and environmental issues more easily and quickly than ever before. Employers compete for talent across the permeable borders of countries around the globe. Prospective and current employees alike are literally wired for greater success as they reach out and engage others and gather information instantly and constantly.

There is an interesting dynamic at play here. While the workforce has indeed shrunk as predictions of 10+ years ago indicated, the shrinkage has not been entirely for the reasons expected (i.e., outsourcing and various forms of retirement). While these are still significant factors, the economic downturn that has forced many employees out of their positions and their companies earlier than expected has added to this shift. As a result, a saturation of talent that is not likely to subside anytime soon has occurred in many disciplines and industries.

Having a global mindset is a key skill required of Trailblazers. It's not a nice to have; it's a *must* have. This is particularly true of those Trailblazers with mature businesses and inclusion and diversity efforts.

# Differences Matter

Being able to engage leaders and employees globally with one unified message of inclusion and diversity is difficult, if not nearly impossible; and perhaps that's as it should be. However, it *is* possible to engage inclusion and diversity from the basis of each organization's core values and make connections between conversations regarding business growth and talent needs. Each region and country has unique challenges. The way U.S. organizations deal with an issue—like disability, for instance—will vary from the way it will be dealt with in India or France in terms of fostering an inclusive culture that optimizes everyone's potential.

That said, each country must determine the most relevant issues around diversity and inclusion for itself. This then becomes the focus for creating critically important and valuable opportunities to its business and its people. Every country's leaders must address the various communities within its workforce and cocreate with the Trailblazer opportunities for advancement of diversity and inclusion that make the most sense for its particular business. A global mindset allows local country leaders to frame, develop, and manage diversity and inclusion as enterprise-wide imperatives for the company in that region. For example, an organization might wish to establish priorities to improve the representation of women at senior levels. The company may set goals at its own level, which each country organization and its local leadership must then define for themselves. They should do so in partnership with their managers, and then determine how they will implement a plan to reduce barriers for women—which they must do in the context of their own local culture.

Despite the fact that many of the Trailblazer companies are headquartered in the United States, a U. S.-centric approach to global diversity is a *definite* deal breaker. As Sodexo Senior Vice President and Global Chief Diversity Officer Rohini Anand points out, "I know what I need to move this work forward; I basically make sure that I position [it] so that it doesn't come across as a specifically 'American' thing. I believe it's the only way to do this work globally. It is challenging, it's difficult, and it takes much longer this way, but I believe that viewing it as a U.S. export immediately creates resistance. Many countries don't think they have issues, and that diversity and inclusion is a U.S. thing that has been thrust down their throats. One of the things I did in

Europe was to actually select someone with no D & I background to manage diversity efforts. He has credibility in the business, and people listen to him because he knows the industry in that country. He's one of "them." I work closely with and through him, because I think the solutions have to come from the countries themselves."

IBM considers it vital for its people to understand what it means to operate in an international environment. The company encourages its employees to become global citizens by volunteering in other countries, learning their cultures, and helping those local governments develop technology solutions free of cost. This does two things for IBM: It gives their people firsthand knowledge of what it means to be a culturally competent global citizen and allows them to understand more about each culture's nuances and how business gets done there. Second, it boosts IBM's ability to cross-pollinate and bring innovative solutions to countries all over the world in a meaningful way.

## Inequality Is Global

Since there is no single, universal definition of *diversity*, it's not surprising that there would be no single, universal definition of *global diversity*. As we've seen, much depends on the issues and challenges that a particular nation or geography faces. One thing is certain, however: Every region of the globe faces inequality. There are places around the world where individuals and even entire groups of people are excluded as human beings. No country is exempt. And, while every region faces these challenges, their specific nature—such as social class, religion, and skin color—varies greatly from one nation to another. They often intersect with conventional dimensions of diversity such as gender, race, disability, and sexual orientation.

Furthermore, topics pertaining to culture, politics, and country laws, for instance, are a large part of this mix. They require leaders to have a very high level of cultural competency, which they achieve most easily by interacting regularly with people from different countries and cultures. A global mindset, then, requires one to think about inclusion and diversity horizontally across various countries, borders, and cultures, and then to deepen the perspective vertically by looking at intracountry cultural issues as well. One must develop a global mindset in inclusion and diversity in order to understand the unique challenges each country faces—to then be able to provide the most relevant talent solutions for that country.

# Generalize; Don't Stereotype

We make no assumptions in conversations regarding global diversity that everyone from a given country is alike simply because they come from that same country. Furthermore, we must recognize that, not only are there differences across cultures, but within them as well—a fact that holds true for the United States as well.

Trailblazers understand that there are common behaviors within each dimension of diversity and each country that are viewed as objective generalizations, and not stereotypes. They utilize these generalizations to provide a framework that allows for common constructs and language for dialogue. It also lets them engage each country individually and address the most significant diversity and inclusion issues for them.

None of the Trailblazers shied away from the term *diversity* as it relates to their global initiatives in our conversations; in fact, they continue to use it even in their global efforts. One might believe that they would instead choose to utilize the term *inclusion*, which many see as a more intuitive and acceptable term—irrespective of the country. We were curious as to why this was the case, since diversity is often thought of as a U.S. concept. We noted that almost all the Trailblazers consider both terms—diversity and inclusion—to be as highly relevant and important in the global arena as in the United States. Their relevance and importance, however, differ depending on the country being considered.

In the fall of 2009, IBM launched a new Global Diversity Strategy that they call Diversity 3.0™. As we talked with Ron, we discovered that IBM has put language to the evolution of this work, in order to give their people a common framework for dialogue and business solutions.

# Journey from Equal Employment Opportunity to Inclusion and Diversity

Many of the Trailblazer companies started with U.S.-focused and -mandated equal employment opportunity in the 1960s and 1970s. The objective at that time was to legally provide underrepresented people—primarily women and people of color—access into corporations, and to track and manage their progress toward certain levels of workforce participation through numerical goals. Companies aimed to eliminate embedded practices of discrimination that were excluding these segments from full participation in the workforce.

However, at the end of the 1970s and during the early 1980s, many organizations recognized that they were not adequately retaining these segments of their workforce. In fact, some had only done the minimum toward developing a respectful and inclusive culture that would help underrepresented employees grow, develop, and contribute to a similar extent as their majority White male counterparts. Clearly, it was just as important for these workforce segments to *know* that the company valued their contributions, and that they *could* advance based on their skills and contributions. As corporations and companies improved their efforts—and as organizations progressed through the 1980s—they began to realize that, while they had noticeably increased representation of underrepresented people, they were woefully lacking in utilizing and keeping these workforce segments. Though they realized that retention was a big problem, this awareness was mostly focused in major U.S. and European markets.

It wasn't until the early 1990s that organizations began to think more about anchoring the concepts of diversity and inclusion together as a long-term change management strategy. Global organizations also began to analyze and discuss these efforts more routinely both inside and outside the United States. However, many multi-national organizations still seemed to view these particular diversity-related issues as a U.S. construct and saw their American counterparts as trying to push these efforts upon them.

Ron Glover shares the following regarding the IBM perspective: "The notion of Diversity 3.0™ says that we can learn and build on some fundamental skills about inclusive environments that create opportunities for people to talk across lines of difference. It allows us to build into organizations the shorthand expression of meritocracies more so than has historically been the case. What really matters is performance and capability in terms of where and how high up in the organization you go. We at IBM decided that, if we're really going to think about this globally, then there are issues that we have to drive and manage as global enterprise-wide imperatives around particular constituencies and communities. We realized that we had to enable local organizations and leaders to define for themselves what they wanted to focus on, and that they needed to localize and define the issues we defined for them as global in order for them to address it effectively within their regions. Diversity 3.0™ recognizes that diversity isn't exclusively about historically excluded or disadvantaged groups. You can't make this global merely by pronouncing it as global. You have to bring folks to the table who *are* global to define this work in ways that are meaningful to them."

Trailblazers accelerate global diversity and inclusion by recognizing country-specific multicultural issues and employing approaches that are relevant for each particular country.

## Customers Exercise Their Choices

Today, organizations large and small can compete with each other across the globe; technology and the speed of information transfer makes it possible to do so. Every day, customers everywhere make decisions about which company to buy product from or which team to work with based on who they feel has their best interest in mind. When all other things are equal, consumers choose companies that they feel can (1) offer products and services that meet their regional needs, and (2) offer cultural astuteness and trusting relationships with their company. Customers often prefer to have cost-competitive products that come from regions of the country they know best and that fit their local requirements. Customers want to deal with companies and employees who understand and speak their specific language; this matters to them. They also want products and people who understand their particular demographic.

As Deborah Dagit, Vice President and Chief Diversity Officer for Merck, explains, "Our diversity and inclusion strategy—which includes our global constituency group as well as our employee resource groups—provides a communications channel for both our employees and their social networks that can let us know about the needs of different populations on a global and regional basis. This allows us to provide critical intelligence to various parts of our business. We have ten global constituency groups that collectively represent our global workforce. They give us a lot of practical experience around leveraging employee information to inform our strategies."

Again, all other things being equal, the organizations with the best product—and those that have most effectively adapted to the local and regional nuances—will be the attractive choice for a potential customer. They are also the ones with whom current customers will want to continue to do business based on a trusted relationship. Customers therefore will select the company and transact with those organizations that they feel understand their specific needs in the context of their culture. Companies are striving to differentiate themselves through customer service; they know that customers want to work with teams with whom they share commonalities and whom they can trust.

## Global Diversity and Talent Management

We'd be remiss if we didn't emphasize the importance of generational issues in the context of global talent competition. This cannot be underestimated, as generational issues related to talent management strongly impact how employees and employers work together around the globe. Large global organizations—like the ones our Trailblazers lead—are forced to go head to head with smaller organizations for talent. The ubiquitous and profound impact of the Internet, social networking, and viral marketing makes it possible for these smaller companies to have a larger footprint and market presence. Corporations that understand this aspect of marketing are much more likely to encounter professional talent because they will mass customize their presence and products based on country-specific differences and preferences. This in turn makes them highly relevant and more in sync with their customer needs around the world. Their ability to be relevant to a broader set of prospective customers and candidates for employment in each particular region gives that organization a competitive advantage. Today's potential employees—irrespective of generation—are drawn to companies with a performance culture of agility, flexibility, a reputation for being less hierarchical, and a greater appreciation of *how* work gets done, not where. Current and prospective workers alike have virtually tipped the scales by demanding that organizations provide challenging work, community involvement, *and* flexibility. And, contrary to conventional thinking, these requirements do not belong to Generation X and Y alone. In fact, Baby Boomers—a group that had traditionally focused heavily on work, perhaps even to the detriment of their personal lives—have become increasingly concerned about work/life blending, health and fitness related issues, and corporate responsibility in recent years.

# Accelerating Results

Trailblazers work with and through others to increase the number of interactions with their employees, prospective clients, customers, and vendors around the world. Today's successful organizations are more adept at working across lines of differences, appreciating similarities, and responding to their people and customers' expectations in meaningful ways. This approach is accelerating results in forward-thinking organizations around the globe; Trailblazers have been a driving force behind this increased awareness.

Rohini Anand of Sodexo explains that Sodexo's global business strategy is focused in three areas: (1) talent excellence, (2) operational excellence, and (3) business excellence. "We know that when we do this well, diversity has to be a competitive advantage and a differentiator to help us grow our business."

---

**INCLUSION INSIGHTS**

**Global Diversity**

- Acknowledge the additional complexity of global diversity.
- Be a curious learner. Effective global diversity efforts are anchored in the knowledge of regional and local leaders. Suspend judgment, and ask, ask, ask.
- Recognize that one size does not fit all. Inter- and intra-country-specific understanding and priorities are required. Think in terms of generalizations, not stereotypes.
- Understand the regional and local environment for politics and laws that might impede or enhance diversity and inclusion implementation.
- Realize that a Western or U.S.-centric approach to global diversity does not work.

---

# 11

# Marketplace/Brand Eminence

Trailblazer companies have highly recognizable brands, some of which have existed for more than 100 years. But how does inclusion and diversity relate to brand eminence in the marketplace? How does this aspect of marketing come into the mix, and what impact does it have?

Throughout this book, we've discussed the ways in which inclusion and diversity influence an organization's systems, culture, and people. We've looked a great deal at the internal influence of elements such as CEO commitment, advisory councils, professional development, metrics, and accountability. These topics and the others we've covered up to this point are integrally involved and absolutely critical to advancing and sustaining inclusion and diversity efforts.

Trailblazers maintain that each organization's reputation in the broader marketplace has a lot to do with its ability to attract new and retain existing talent. The credibility that outsiders afford the company—the "street cred," as some call it—speaks volumes about the organization. It indicates whether the company is considered a magnet for talented prospective employees to flock to join and one that current employees feel proud to be a part of—or whether the word on the street is unfavorable or downright negative. Such a reputation would likely deter potential employees and decrease

**153**

employee moral for those employees who remain at the company for whatever their reasons.

Whatever side of the equation you choose, you can be certain that the organization's "street cred" and reputation will affect its ability to meet its business objectives for talent. Obviously, the key is to be on the plus side of the ledger.

The Trailblazers' organizations have long-standing histories—perhaps even legacies—of being "top employers" in the world and/or their industries. In fact, several of the Trailblazer companies are listed on Fortune's Top 50 World's Most Admired Companies 2010, and several others make the list of Fortune's 346 Most Admired Companies in the World. Though these are clearly significant accomplishments for each of these organizations in and of themselves, they also carry significant weight in that the ratings come from corporate executives, not consumers.

## Relationship of Inclusion and Diversity to the Marketplace

Trailblazers intimately know their brand's value and impact. One Trailblazer in particular shared an eye-opening account of how the influence of diversity and inclusion has put her organization on the map—so to speak—and in top standing with prospective employees. Rohini Anand of Sodexo shared with us what it has meant to the business.

Rohini began by saying that Sodexo is not really a well-known brand in the United States. In fact, as she claims, "People didn't know who Sodexo was or what we did; they couldn't even pronounce the company name. Over the years, however—through the efforts of our Diversity and Inclusion leadership engaging the organization in culture changes and telling the story internally and externally—Sodexo became recognized in the marketplace for its leadership. People would tell us that they wanted to come and work for Sodexo because it's a D & I leader—but would then ask us, 'What does Sodexo do?' So really, D & I led Sodexo's branding externally by way of becoming successful internally. It became a differentiator for us, and something that we could share with our clients. That's something that companies pay millions of dollars for."

An organization that has a reputation as a successful D & I leader is attractive to prospective employees and clients alike. More and more companies today want to do business with organizations that have similarly effective D & I efforts and talent pipelines that reflect today's diverse labor force. Organizations are very much aware that their constituents—customers, vendors, potential and current staff members—pay close attention to how the organization "talks the talk" and "walks the walk" with its inclusion and diversity efforts.

Companies these days are increasingly interested in doing business with organizations that hold views regarding inclusion and diversity that are similar to their own. As a former CDO, I witnessed firsthand the number of requests for proposals (RFPs) skyrocket. They came from companies with well-known brands and highly recognizable logos, who often requested very specific information—including numerical data—on inclusion and diversity efforts' effectiveness. These requests require a delineation of information that provides a representative and clear picture of D & I initiatives' progress and effectiveness. They were seeking substantive information.

The requests often covered such areas as: internal and marketplace communications collateral; information on training delivered, topics covered, and number trained; percentages of supplier diversity spending by category for women, minorities, and veterans; number and types of employee resource groups; and the history of advancement of women and people of color at certain levels. There was never any question as to whether there would be compliance with the RFP information requests from these companies. They represented significant possible revenue should the contract be won, as well as a continuing mutually productive relationship and existing revenue when the contract was renewed.

It is important to note that the majority of RFP requests for inclusion and diversity information *did not* come from governmental agencies or accounts. While we expected that these kinds of groups would require and would receive such information, they represented only a relatively small fraction of RFPs. The majority of requests came from publicly traded organizations—those with a vested interest in inclusion and diversity success primarily because of their own efforts. We also observed that these organizations wanted to ensure that they were working with companies whose approach enhanced their own efforts. Many had boards and shareholders who had become increasingly vigilant and vocal regarding improved inclusion and diversity progress.

The meaning here is twofold. When organizations have a noticeable gap between what they claim to be committed to doing and what they actually do, unfavorable comments travel very fast. In addition, this can negatively impact their reputation in the marketplace, thereby affecting relationships with prospective customers and employees, and within the workforce. The flip side, however, is also true. Each of these areas can impact the bottom line in a favorable way.

We've observed that it's hard to turn on the TV today and not see a show where people are being evaluated and judged by a panel of experts on some given topic—just pick your favorite. Organizations certainly operate in this way and are also accustomed to being evaluated by boards and shareholders. Today, they're evaluated and publicized constantly as progressive Best Companies for *this* award, or Worst Company for *that* award. This phenomenon has occurred so much over the last eight to ten years that organizations are now requesting to be evaluated on their inclusiveness and diversity profiles as well. One reason they do this is to get the anonymous and confidential benchmark data from which to continue to internally evaluate themselves against their competitive standing in the marketplace. Another aim is to make external constituencies aware that they are actively seeking to make tangible improvements in their inclusion and diversity efforts. They want their customers' appreciation of this progress to favorably impact their brand in the marketplace.

It is highly desirable for companies to be ranked and favorably profiled for their inclusion and diversity efforts by organizations and magazines such as Catalyst, Hispanic Business, Diversity Inc., Black Enterprise, *Fortune*, *Working Mother*, and *Business Week*—just to name a few. This speaks volumes to the marketplace regarding the brand and the efforts of those organizations, and it implies that they have indeed made significant accomplishments that should be recognized and rewarded. Being profiled as a Top 10, 50, or 100 is attention getting and newsworthy. It lets the industry as a whole—and, specifically, your competitors—know just how serious your organization is about improving in these key areas. It may also let your existing employees know that their organization is making real progress that is being recognized.

# Evaluations and Recognitions: Double-Edged Swords?

There's been an increase in the popularity of many evaluating organizations and magazines lately due to the much publicized "events" that they use to highlight the best organizations. In our view, however, this has become a double-edged sword.

On the one side, there is of course the well-deserved recognition for efforts on the part of showcased company members. Given the nature of the inclusion and diversity work, the external marketplace tends to appreciate the work accomplished more than the internal population does. This demonstration of gratitude is so important to those doing this work that it becomes part of the incentive to continue doing it.

On the other hand, what the evaluating organization considers important may not be where your particular company should focus. Maintaining clear purpose and objectives for your organization's specific D & I strategy and efforts must take priority in the minds of senior leadership. There comes a point when, after appearing on such lists again and again, some companies tend to lose focus on the most critical elements of *their* business—and instead become unwittingly preoccupied with the evaluating organization's criteria for recognition. These two groups of elements, after all, may or may not be the same thing. It would be a travesty to set your company's objectives based on someone or something other than senior leadership's focus and your business objectives. We therefore submit that inclusion and diversity strategies remain "evergreen," and that organizations revisit the business relevancy frequently. This way, you can ensure that it supports the business plans for reasons that are important to your talent acquisition and retention, business growth, and sustainability strategies.

# Making the Words and the Music Match

As most Trailblazers will tell you, it can be a challenge to balance the internal and the external communications about their companies. While this complexity applies to any major company message, it is particularly true—and somewhat sensitive—in regard to the topic of inclusion and diversity. One of the greatest challenges that a Trailblazer can face takes place when the external "buzz" about their organization's inclusion and diversity efforts is granted greater importance and is ahead of what employees believe, understand, or feel to be true.

As organizations have come to more fully appreciate the value of D & I initiatives, many have realized just how important employee engagement surveys can be as an anonymous means for gathering feedback on the effectiveness of these efforts. This tool provides credible information as to whether—and where—employees feel their organization is advancing with inclusion and diversity efforts.

Trailblazers conduct employee engagement surveys regularly. Several of their companies have developed sections with D & I-specific questions within the larger survey that highlight inclusion and diversity issues and successes. They use these sections to understand what is working, which, in turn, enables Trailblazers and their organizations to identify what interventions need to be made to remedy key issues, and with what segments of their workforce. The survey provides a clear picture of which areas, levels, people, and practices are impacting their various constituencies—both favorably and unfavorably. The objective data that employee engagement surveys provide—and the ability to communicate these results back to staff members on a timely basis—keep both employees and leaders informed of the challenges and progress of inclusion and diversity. It's also a key means to ensuring that the behaviors support the talk, or that the words and the music of the organization match.

Company reputation matters. As organizations attempt to stabilize from the recent dramatic changes in the economy, the rankings of who is admired most and for what can be an important differentiator in today's talent market.

---

### INCLUSION INSIGHTS

#### Marketplace Brand Eminence

- Brand matters.
- Inclusion and diversity can be a key differentiator in the marketplace.

- Brand and reputation affect talent acquisition and retention.
- Companies want to do business with other companies that appreciate the importance of inclusion and diversity.
- RFPs are increasingly incorporating information regarding inclusion and diversity efforts, information, and progress.
- External recognition can be an asset or a liability.
- Employee engagement surveys are an important means of obtaining unbiased information regarding what employees *really* think about inclusion and diversity.
- And of course . . . brand matters!

As a closing thought, we'd like to touch on the issue of corporate sponsorships as they relate to branding and reputation in the marketplace. Trailblazers recognize that these programs are an important means of fueling the talent pipeline. Maintaining a presence as a supporter of particular associations and national professional organizations allows companies to make certain that the external world knows where they stand on developing and acquiring people. This is particularly important given the workforce challenges for experienced professional workers. From well-placed advertisements in trade magazines, to billboards lining airport terminal walls, to web sites, organizations spend millions of dollars to showcase their brand, people, and products—hoping that this exposure will help attract the talent necessary to grow. Hundreds of thousands of dollars are also spent to support constituency-based professional membership associations and national organizations—such as the Human Rights Campaign or the National Association of Hispanic Engineers—for this same reason. In some cases, these membership organizations can potentially provide an ongoing stream of candidates to the Trailblazer organizations over time. In other cases, they're able to forge relationships between certain companies with their constituencies as targeted employers of their skills and talents. None of this happens without partnership.

Trailblazers spend time with and view these organizations and universities as partners in the recruitment efforts for potential talent. They make sure that these groups—many of which are 501c3 or tax exempt organizations—understand that the companies' hiring profiles require both experienced workers and college graduates. Trailblazers collaborate with these associations' executive directors and CEOs to continually inform them of their talent needs. They make connections between which associations receive their company's active support as a means of identifying and potentially fueling their talent pipeline. Those organizations that aren't able to fulfill the company's talent requirements are unlikely to receive the continued commitment of time and funding dollars, if there is little to no ROI for the business.

We've witnessed a marked decline in sponsorship budgets over the last few years. Spending is being scrutinized and becoming an increasingly smaller percentage of inclusion and diversity budgets overall. Therefore, universities and professional and national organizations that don't demonstrate the capacity to help identify talented people—and/or use their influence to help companies develop key skills and expertise in prospective employees—are likely to be dismissed.

# 12

# And the Research Says. . .

## *Facts vs. Myths*

---

*"Equal employment opportunity remains elusive for far too many workers . . . employers must step up their efforts to foster discrimination-free and inclusive workplaces, or risk enforcement and litigation by the EEOC."*
—Acting EEOC Chair Stuart J. Ishimaru, 2010

## Introduction

Many employers have made significant efforts, having spent millions of dollars on diversity initiatives, yet charges of discrimination in the workplace continue to grow. It appears that leaders of many organizations honestly want to create an inclusive workplace where all employees can be productive but the best ideas about how to leverage diversity and, equally as important, inclusion, remains apparently elusive for some.

Research team: E. Holly Buttner, PhD, Kevin B. Lowe, PhD, and Lenora Billings-Harris, Bryan School of Business and Economics, University of North Carolina-Greensboro.

We set out, through a series of research projects spanning almost 10 years, to address some of the issues surrounding effective management of the organizational diversity climate. Some of the questions we have addressed are:

- Are managers of color the best leaders of diversity initiatives?
- Is it all about the money for employees of color?
- Are all employees sensitive to diversity climate issues?
- What is the impact of diversity climate on employee of color outcomes: job satisfaction, organizational commitment, performance, and turnover intentions?

We summarized what we learned during this past decade of research into various aspects of diversity management, particularly with respect to leadership of diversity initiatives and the impact of dimensions of the diversity climate on outcomes for professional employees of color.

## Are Leaders of Color the Best Leaders of Diversity Initiatives?

Managers of color leading diversity initiatives in organizations play an important and a symbolic role. Through their presence, they can represent the importance the organization places on effective diversity and inclusion leadership. They also imply inherent life experiences and an enhanced awareness of the issues and challenges faced by underrepresented groups within the organization. In essence, a manager's ethnicity can symbolize a company's racial awareness. What is also interesting to note is that previous studies have used both gender and race as defining characteristics regarding racial attitudes.[1]

This raised an interesting concept about whether White male managers could also lead diversity initiatives in organizations effectively. What makes the difference in diversity leadership? Is it gender, ethnicity, or a leader's racial awareness that affects his or her attitude toward diversity? Of course, racial awareness theory suggests the latter to be the dominant factor. Attitudes and awareness about diversity exist along a consistent path, but they can change and evolve over time.[2]

Dr. Janet Helms developed a model of racial identity awareness that proposed that racial awareness is a developmental process; it begins with a lack of awareness of one's own racial identity and limited exposure to those who are different. A more developed but still limited form of identity development is color blindness. This is a cognitive representation used to interpret racial stimuli. A component of color blindness includes the belief that racism is a phenomenon of the past and does not impact U.S. daily life.[3]

There is a higher level of identity development than color blindness, which acknowledges that race does in fact play a role in social relations and that it involves replacing stereotypes with more accurate information.[4] We found through our research that, while a leader's gender and ethnicity did not influence his or her attitude toward diversity, the leader's racial awareness did. Leaders with greater racial awareness, regardless of gender or ethnicity, had more positive attitudes toward diversity. This suggests that, for those seeking to improve organizations through diversity initiatives, it might be best to assess racial awareness in the selection of business and department leaders rather than to base a strategy or decision on surface-level characteristics such as sex or ethnicity.

Following Dr. Helms's model of racial identity awareness, would racial awareness affect leaders' perceptions about the causes of minority underrepresentation and, consequently, the leaders' views of potential solutions? That is, if this theory was correct, leaders with greater racial awareness would be more likely to recognize the underrepresentation of faculty of color as a consequence of institutional racism and may be less likely to attribute underrepresentation to performance-related issues arising from individual differences. After reviewing literature on diversity trends in higher education, it appears that business school leaders' perspectives about the causes of underrepresentation of minority faculty and potential strategies for alleviating the shortage is an important but relatively unexplored domain. It is important, then, to expand on the logic and theory supporting this line of thought.

## Deep-Level Diversity versus Surface-Level Diversity Perspectives

Ruth Frankenberg argued that a dimension of a color-blind racial attitude is "power evasion," which is the belief that every person has the same opportunities to succeed. Individuals holding this power evasion perspective run the risk of making the fundamental attribution error,[5] that sees the individual minority member's failure to succeed as the sole responsibility of that person. A business leader who is unaware of the advantages afforded by majority status might therefore believe that a minority employee's possible low performance was solely determined by the efforts (or lack therof) and abilities of that individual. On the other hand, a leader with greater awareness of the advantages of majority status might be less likely to attribute possible failure exclusively to the individual and to accept that variable factors, such as the availability of mentors for guidance and inclusion in informal networks where critical work-related information is conveyed, also may play a role. Similarly, more racially aware leaders may appreciate that the impact of organizational culture is a more important cause of the shortage of professionals of color than a less racially aware leader may be.

These and other possible effects of racial awareness of the leader compared to leader ethnicity on perceptions and attributions about causes of and solutions to the shortage of professional employees of color (e.g., faculty) in United States business schools were explored.[6] Organization and business leaders who participated in the study were asked to rate the importance of various factors presented in business literature as possible causes of and solutions to the faculty of color shortage experienced by most business schools. Some of the results were surprising. First, it was discovered that business school leader sex and race are not significant predictors of attributed causes and proposed solutions to faculty of color underrepresentation. Leaders of color and female leaders did not rate the causes of or solutions to the employee of color shortage differently than did White male leaders. So, selecting a leader of color or a White female leader of a diversity program does not ensure that the leader will be more sensitive to the diversity climate. In other words, White leaders who are racially aware may be equally as effective as leaders of color.

Overall, of the possible causes of the shortage of professionals of color that were provided, the leader participants rated competition between institutions as the most important cause of the shortage and recruitment of faculty of color as the most important solution. The leaders questioned appeared to believe that time, the second most highly rated solution, will alleviate the underrepresentation of faculty of color in their business schools. Results also indicated that the business school leaders did not view individual performance as an important cause of the shortage but believed performance-related feedback could help improve faculty of color representation.

When the cause of the leaders' ratings as a function of their racial awareness was analyzed, differences emerged. Leaders with greater awareness of racial issues rated organizational culture (e.g., inhospitable culture, exclusion from informal networks, social isolation, overt prejudice and discrimination) as a more important cause of faculty of color underrepresentation than did less racially aware leaders. These differences were statistically significant.

When it comes to solutions to the professional of color shortage, it would stand to reason that leaders who are more racially aware would rate changing the diversity culture in organizations and tactical strategies, such as recruitment and providing high-quality feedback to help minority employees refine their skills to enhance performance, as more important than their less racially aware counterparts. When evaluating the solutions to faculty of color underrepresentation, more racially aware leaders indeed viewed cultural change and recruitment as more important factors in improving these conditions than did their less aware colleagues.

Also, those less aware leaders indicated that individual minority members should take more responsibility for their performance than did the more racially aware participants. Overall, the results suggested that racially aware leaders tend to attribute the causes of and solutions to faculty of color underrepresentation to more systemic factors than personal effort or abilities. This explanation may result in fundamental attribution error that occurs when an observer (in this case, the department leader) attributes the cause of an individual's behavior or performance to that individual when systemic factors may play a more substantive role.

In general, a business school leader's awareness of racial issues (deep-level diversity) had a greater impact on the leader's ratings of various causes of the faculty of color shortage and possible solution strategies than did the surface-level characteristics of race or sex. These findings also suggested that, to increase employee recognition of the value of diversity initiatives, systematic programs to shape racial awareness at the organizational level, beginning with the leader, may prove effective. *These results should be regarded as encouraging as they suggest that enhancing a leader's racial awareness may be more effective than firing and hiring to reshape leader demographics.*

The results of this phase of the first project suggest that business schools need to increase the number of qualified candidates available in the job market by recruiting and graduating a larger number of students of color. Recently reported recruitment initiatives include efforts to recruit high school students to undergraduate business programs[7] and the PhD Project that provides networking, peer support, mentoring, and joint research opportunities for minority doctoral students. However, active recruitment of faculty of color without increasing the supply may perpetuate increases in salaries for highly trained faculty of color as schools compete for the same small number of qualified candidates, which is discussed in the next section.

## Universities Employing Professionals of Color: What Are Their Results?

Various arguments have appeared in the business press about the business reasons for enhancing diversity in organizations' workforces. What are the arguments for enhancing diversity in U.S. business schools? Minority representation in business school faculty is important for several reasons. First, a small but growing number of business students are from minority groups. Faculty of color can serve as role models for students from all racial/ethnic groups. Second, having a diverse faculty is important for competitive reasons. Research has shown that well-managed problem-solving teams with diverse membership develop higher quality solutions.[8] These teams integrate a broader range of perspectives and enable organizations to consider various stakeholders' interests in responding to the environment. For business schools, this may mean having a larger applicant pool from which to select its student body as well as a faculty that more effectively responds to a global environment.

## Strategic Priorities of Diversity and Inclusion

Figure 12.1 summarizes data pertaining to the strategic priority of diversity in participating business schools and at their universities. Leaders indicated that, while diversity was a moderately important strategic priority in terms of mission and objective statements at the

**This table reports the strategic priority of diversity at participatinng institutions as well as factors that could affect these priorities.**

| **1** Lowest strategic importance | ▌ ▐ ▐ █ █ █ █ █ █ █ | **5** Highest strategic importance |
|---|---|---|

| Result Average | Items |
|---|---|
| 3.83 | 1. Please rate the strategic priority of diversity at the **university** level of your university or college as evidenced by mission and objectives statements and other formal documents. |
| 3.27 | 2. Please rate the strategic priority of diversity at the **university** level of your university or college as evidenced by commitment of resources. |
| 3.54 | 3. Please rate the strategic priority of diversity at your **business school** as evidenced by mission and objectives statements and other formal documents. |
| 3.30 | 4. Please rate the strategic priority of diversity at your **business school** as evidenced by commitment of resources. |

| No control | Some | Moderate | Considerable | Extensive control |
|---|---|---|---|---|
| 1 | 2 | 3 | 4 | 5 |

| 3.54 | 5. How much authority do you have to implement diversity initiatives in your **business school**? |
|---|---|

| No control | Some | Moderate | Considerable | Extensive control |
|---|---|---|---|---|
| 1 | 2 | 3 | 4 | 5 |

| 2.15 | 6. To what extent is the successful implementation of diversity initiatives a part of your annual performance review conducted by your superior? |
|---|---|

| No pressure | Some | Moderate | Considerable | Great pressure |
|---|---|---|---|---|
| 1 | 2 | 3 | 4 | 5 |

| 2.36 | 7. How much pressure do you feel from constituencies (e.g. Business advisory boards, employers, other Deans, or other stakeholders) outside the university to implement diversity strategies in your **business school**? |
|---|---|

**FIGURE 12.1**  **Strategic Priority of Diversity**

institutional level, they perceived that the priority ranked lower when it came to allocating of resources. In the business schools, diversity was rated slightly lower in importance in mission and objective statements but about the same as the university priority in allocation of resources.

Participants reported that they had a moderate to considerable degree of authority to implement diversity initiatives in their schools. However, diversity was a minor part of the criteria used to evaluate the performance of participants. Finally, respondents indicated that they felt moderate pressure from constituents outside the university to implement diversity strategies.

## Type and Extent of Diversity Activities

The type and extent of diversity activities reported by university leaders is shown in Figure 12.2. The most common components were a strategic plan emphasizing recruitment and retention of minorities, mentoring of faculty from underrepresented groups, and communication of the school's commitment to diversity in various publications. A majority of the leaders also reported that their universities routinely compare racial demographics of their faculty, conduct exit interviews of departing faculty, and have advisory boards representative of their local community's diversity. Few leaders reported that their schools were going beyond these initiatives.

While the majority of schools emphasize diversity and inclusion in mission statements, few have formal written goals for increasing faculty diversity or a formal system to monitor progress toward achieving representation goals. There was also a small percentage of schools that had a diversity component in the performance review of administrators or who hold administrators, such as department heads, accountable for achieving representation goals. A small percentage of schools have a committee to monitor the school diversity climate. Similarly, while demographics are routinely measured, faculty satisfaction by ethnicity is not. A fairly common diversity initiative among participating schools was diversity training, but a smaller percentage indicated that administrators, including department heads, participated in it. Finally, less than half of responding schools celebrate diversity through school events.

This table reports on diversity activities at participant schools. Respondents indicated agreement with each statement. Responses are summarized below:

| Item Number | Items | Strongly Disagree/ Disagree | Neither | Agree/ Strongly Agree |
|---|---|---|---|---|
| | | Percent (%) | % | % |
| 1 | The strategic plan emphasizes the goal of recruiting and retaining a workforce representative of the business school student body's racial/ethnic demographics. | 12 | 29 | 59 |
| 2 | My business school has effective formal written goals and timetables for increasing the number of minority faculty and administrators. | 57 | 24 | 19 |
| 3 | A standing committee (task force, action council) monitors the business school's diversity climate. | 64 | 15 | 21 |
| 4 | Racial/ethnic demographics of the faculty are routinely compared by level (Professor, Associate, Assistant, and Instructor) by school administrators. | 32 | 18 | 50 |
| 5 | Faculty satisfaction is routinely evaluated and compared among racial/ethnic groups. | 72 | 19 | 9 |
| 6 | My business school has a formal system that effectively monitors the progress for accomplishing its diversity goals. | 44 | 28 | 28 |
| 7 | Administrators are held accountable for achieving specific diversity goals at my business school.goals. | 56 | 22 | 22 |
| 8 | My business school includes a diversity component in the performance review of administrators. | 58 | 21 | 21 |
| 9 | My business school offers (or has offered) diversity training to support its goals. | 41 | 10 | 49 |
| 10 | Administrators and department heads actively participate in diversity training. | 43 | 26 | 31 |
| 11 | Formal mentoring programs for new faculty members are emphasized. | 14 | 14 | 73 |
| 12 | Activities to celebrate diverse racial/ethnic heritages are conducted in the business school. | 42 | 21 | 37 |
| 13 | My business school has explicitly communicated (e.g. memos, public announcements, promotional materials) its commitment to diversity. | 13 | 20 | 67 |
| 14 | Exit interviews are routinely conducted when faculty members leave. | 23 | 23 | 54 |
| 15 | The board of business advisors for the business school represents the racial/ethnic diversity of the overall community. | 26 | 24 | 5 |

**FIGURE 12.2** U.S. Business School Study Participant Diversity Activities

While it appears that business school leaders recognize the importance of diversity on their faculties, the number of schools with actionable tactics is fairly small. Recruitment of faculty of color may remain a challenge for the foreseeable future until the supply of faculty of color increases. This shortage may exert upward pressure on the salaries of faculty of color.

## Is It All about the Money for Employees of Color?

While people of color are moving into the ranks of organizations in increasing numbers, they are often still underrepresented, particularly in the managerial ranks of most U.S. organizations, and including business schools. Why would that be?

Various possible causes have been proposed in business literature. Some of these ideas suggest that low minority-group representation is due to leader racial insensitivity and discrimination. Another line of reasoning is that there is a small pipeline of professionals of color. A third possible cause is that there are unequal opportunities for women and people of color. Economic theory also predicts that faculty of color act rationally in order to maximize personal outcomes in choosing among employment opportunities; that is, they go to the highest paying organization. Finally, it is argued that organizational leaders, while claiming that diversity in their organization's workforce is important, actually place low strategic priority on diverse workforce representation. All of these ideas seem reasonable. However, there is little research that has been conducted to examine whether any or all of these possible causes explain the underrepresentation of people of color. We set out to answer this question.

In a survey taken by business school deans, we asked them to indicate the percent of full-time U.S.-born men and women of color and White women they had on their faculty. We used this statistic to determine which, if any, of the arguments presented above predicted minority faculty employment levels.

We found some intriguing results. Leaders who indicated greater racial awareness had higher representation of minority and women faculty in their departments. Leaders who rated cultural change as more important also had higher minority-group and women representation than their colleagues who reported that cultural change was of lower importance. Interestingly, when we accounted for the ratings of cultural change, leader racial awareness was no longer a significant predictor of minority representation. This showed that, when a leader appreciates the importance of changing his or her organization's culture, their personal racial awareness is not as important in affecting minority-group representation.

We also found that the strategic priority of diversity did not predict faculty of color representation. Instead, leaders' appreciation of the importance of the more specific strategies of minority recruitment and provision of performance-related feedback predicted minority-group representation. Thus, it appears that it is not the assignment of a high strategic priority to diversity that matters; it is the action-oriented tactics that have an impact on diverse representation on school faculties.

The profit maximization economics theory that faculty of color would behave rationally and be more highly represented at higher-paying institutions was not supported. Instead, there was a negative relationship between pay and minority-group representation. Other research suggests that employees of color at institutions of higher learning may be sensitive to pay levels, so the relationship between pay levels and minority-group representation appears to be more complicated than originally considered.[9] Later research project findings suggest that professionals of color are sensitive to other aspects of the employment relationship, including the organization's diversity climate. These other factors may interact with or override the importance of pay in faculty of color employment decisions. More on this later.

# Are All Employees Sensitive to Diversity Climate Issues?

Recall that, in our earlier work studying unit leaders' attitudes toward diversity, we found that racial awareness was a significant predictor. More racially aware leaders were more sensitive to the effects of diversity climate on the causes of and solutions to the shortage of professionals of color in their departments. In a second project, research was expanded to focus on professionals from underrepresented groups on business school faculties. In addition, other diversity scholars have examined the attitudes of both White employees and employees of color concerning the diversity climates in their organizations.

In perhaps the earliest study of perceptions of the diversity climate, it was discovered that, compared to White men, White women and racial/ethnic minorities valued employer efforts to promote diversity more highly and held more positive attitudes about the qualifications of women and racio-ethnic minority-group members.[10] It was also reported that Caucasian men perceived their organizations as more fair and inclusive than did Caucasian women and racial/ethnic minority men and women.[11] The members from minority racial groups as well as the Caucasian women reported greater value in diversity than did the Caucasian male participants.

A more recent study found that Black employees were more sensitive to managerial behavioral integrity than members of any other racial group.[12] Interestingly, the Black participants in the study appeared to rate the behavioral integrity of Black managers more severely than they did White managers. It was speculated that this result could be due to the expectations held by Black employees of their Black supervisors to provide positive treatment, support for Black issues in the organization, or recognition of their concerns and issues.

The diversity climate has been defined in a variety of ways in diversity literature. Dr. Chrobot-Mason developed one definition that focused on promises or expectations that employees of color might have about their organizations. Her conceptualization of diversity promises included diverse representation in the company workforce, consideration of minority members' input in decision making, valuing diverse opinions, and elimination of racial bias. She found that employees of color perceived diversity promises to be distinct from general organizational promises. While employees of color valued diversity promises as highly as general organizational promises, such as career development, they reported that, in their experience, diversity promises were less likely to be met.

In an interesting study of employee descriptions of diversity incidents in one large U.S. organization, Roberson and Stevens found that a common theme pertained to the diversity climate.[13] The study participants were 70 percent male and 80 percent White, suggesting that White employees are sensitive to diversity climate issues. Hopkins, Hopkins, and Malette reported that, in their study of White male managers and managers of color, perceptions of their organization's commitment to diversity was perceived by both groups of managers as a positive factor in the workplace.[14] It appears then that White employees might also appreciate the positive effect of an inviting, diverse workplace.

# The Impact of Diversity on Climate for Employees of Color and the Outcomes

## Job Satisfaction, Organizational Commitment, Performance, and Turnover Intentions

Before examining the effect of the diversity climate, it is useful to consider a broader question: Does the organizational climate affect employee outcomes such as satisfaction with and commitment to their organization, psychological well-being, performance, or turnover intentions? A meta-analysis of the effects of employees' organizational climate perceptions on their work outcomes was conducted by Carr, Schmidt, Ford, and DeShon.[15] A meta-analysis is a statistical technique for combining the results of a large number of studies to draw overall conclusions. Meta-analyses highlight the general patterns evidenced in the research. Carr and her colleagues found that employees' perceptions of their organizational climates impacted job satisfaction and organizational commitment, which, in turn, influenced job performance, psychological well-being, and withdrawal. A related study of the effect of climate at the organizational and department levels found that, while organizational climate accounted for a large percentage of the variance in employees' job satisfaction, unit level climate accounted for a small but significant portion of job satisfaction variance above and beyond that explained by the organizational climate.[16]

This research indicates that it is useful for organizational leaders to pay attention to the nature of their organization's climate and its impact on organizational members. Does the more nuanced aspect of climate, specifically diversity climate, affect employee outcomes? Several researchers set out to address this question.

Hicks-Clarke and Iles examined the effect of diversity climate perceptions on employees' work outcomes and found that climate perceptions affected organizational commitment and job satisfaction.[17] This suggested that climate dimensions might have an important effect on retention of professional employees. However, these researchers did not examine the perceptions of participants of color. Other research has confirmed that the nature of the climate affects employees of color work outcomes. Two studies have focused on and demonstrated that organizational diversity climate affects employee of color outcomes, including job satisfaction, cynicism, and assessments of organizational attractiveness.[18]

Based on previous findings of department leaders and on the literature on racial awareness, the relationship between perceptions of diversity promise fulfillment and racial awareness on employees' of color reports of psychological contract violation was explored.[19] First, it must begin with an explanation of the psychological contract.

A *psychological contract* is defined as the employee's belief about obligations or inferred promises between the employee and his/her employing organization (rather than between the employee and organizational agents).[20] Psychological contracts are both perceptual and idiosyncratic in nature. Tangible dimensions of the psychological contract may include effort, experience, expertise, and commitment provided by the employee in exchange for compensation and benefits. The psychological contract may also include employee expectations about intangible dimensions regarding the organizational climate and the nature of treatment by organizational agents, particularly the employee's direct supervisor.[21]

One potentially important dimension of the psychological contract for employees of color pertains to expectations about the diversity climate of the employing organization. For employees of color, fulfillment of the psychological contract on the part of the employer may include employer obligations and commitments to provide a positive and supportive diversity climate.[22] It was found that employees of color who expected their employers to provide a positive diversity climate would report a lower commitment to their employer if it was perceived that their employers had not fulfilled those obligations or that promise. Furthermore, racially aware professionals of color who perceived that their organizations had not fulfilled diversity promises reported greater psychological contract violation.

It was also important to learn whether two aspects of organizational climate, organizational justice and diversity climate, interacted to influence employee outcomes: organizational commitment and turnover intentions. It was discovered that, to generate high levels of organizational commitment for professional employees of color, managers should pay attention to the fairness of organizational processes and procedures. Managers also need to ensure that diversity climate promises are honored. Treating professionals of color with respect appears to be ineffective when basic organizational and diversity climate promises go unfulfilled.

Other research contributes additional information about the effect of diversity climate on employee outcomes. A study of the effect of diversity climate on turnover intentions of managers in 743 stores of a large retail organization in the United States found that, while pro-diversity climate perceptions were associated with lower turnover intentions across all racial groups, the diversity climate effect was significantly stronger for Black employees than for White or Hispanic employees.[23]

An intriguing follow-up study examined the relationship between diversity climate and sales performance.[24] It found that, while the performance of White employees was unaffected by the diversity climate, Black and Hispanic employees had greater increases in sales per hour in stores with a pro-diversity climate.

In summary, the research that has been conducted suggests that the diversity climate plays an influential role in employee outcomes, including perceptions of psychological contract violation, commitment to the organizations, (sales) performance, and intentions to leave. In this next section, we share some lessons that come from research regarding the effect of diversity climate on organizational performance.

## Research Setting: U.S. Business Schools

One of the primary training grounds in the United States for new business entrants is business schools, which served as the setting for many of these studies. Business schools are of interest for several reasons. First, among divisions in universities, business schools are most like business organizations in values, culture, and expertise. Additionally, faculty in business schools are highly trained and educated. Recruitment and retention of professionals is an ongoing challenge in most U.S. organizations, so the findings could provide insight about how organizations employing professionals might address the challenge of managing diverse professional groups. Finally, while students of color have enrolled in increasing numbers at many U.S. universities, they have made less progress in schools of business. We turn to statistics to provide background regarding the diversity status of U.S. business schools.

African American, Hispanic, Asian American, Native American, and other minority-group members have enrolled at U.S. colleges and universities in increasing numbers over the past two decades. These groups constituted 28 percent of college students in 2000 (U.S. Department of Education, 2002). However, according to the DOE (2002), only 14 percent of U.S. faculty in colleges and universities were minority-group members in 1999. In 2002 to 2003, African Americans, Hispanics, Asian Americans, and Native Americans constituted only 17 percent of undergraduate students and 8 percent of MBA students in U.S. business schools.[25] Since business schools are suppliers of business talent for U.S. corporations, and people of color in general are underrepresented in universities, this industry was particularly well-suited for exploration. For more information about the statistics summarizing the leader participant sample and the faculty of color sample, please see the Appendix.

The second project shifted to the other side of the equation, surveying professionals of color, specifically faculty of color in accredited U.S. business schools. We were fortunate to have the support and endorsement of the PhD Project, a networking organization that mentors aspiring business PhD candidates and provides post-graduation networking opportunities for faculty of color in the United States. This project was particularly interested in U.S.-born faculty of color who make up the majority of the membership of the PhD Project but who are still underrepresented at most U.S. business schools.

# Research Summary

When we began this series of research projects nearly a decade ago, our interest was in exploring the ingredients, the "special sauce," so to speak, of an effective diversity climate. To do this, we measured the attitudes and perspectives of the leaders who control the levers for effecting these changes and then we surveyed the employees who are the recipients of these climate-oriented initiatives. So did we learn anything, or did we, as academic research in the social sciences is sometimes accused, take elaborate steps to prove the obvious? Our own answer to this question is that we did learn some new things; we now also better understand some of the mechanisms by which an effective climate is accomplished; and we reassured ourselves that other widely held hunches were indeed verifiable with good science. Some of the important conclusions that have been drawn include the following:

- Organizations that are effective at managing minority employees consider the full employee life cycle. Our review of the literature suggests that organizations have become much more adept at identifying applicants and attracting minority employees to their organizations. They appear to be much less adept at managing minority employee experiences once they are inside the organization or learning from their mistakes. On this latter point, one quick test for an organization would be to answer: Do you investigate aspects of the diversity climate in exit interviews? If the answer is no, an important continuous improvement opportunity is being lost.

- If you want to build an affirming climate for diverse employees, look past the surface-level diversity when choosing your leadership team and focus on a more sophisticated measurement of the racial awareness of that team. Symbolic appointments are just that—symbolic—and if real organizational change is the goal, subordinate physical appearance to racial awareness in choosing the leadership team. A corollary is that, if you have a team in place that lacks racial awareness, start by developing their racial awareness before rolling out programs to lower levels of the organization.

- Leaders who are effective at changing the diversity climate frame the challenge as a systemic challenge, and an organizational culture challenge. Leaders who are less effective see the challenge as more individual employee based. While this might appear to be common sense at first glance, it is not so common when we consider what occurs within many well-intentioned organizations. An organization leader (e.g., Business School Dean) might actually want to improve the climate for minority and women employees and communicate that each line manager (e.g., Department Head) should seek to provide a more hospitable environment for minority and women employees. But such an approach would fail the systemic test and results in a series of disjointed efforts that lack integration and reinforcement throughout the system.

- Leaders who have "development of an affirming diversity climate" as a significant portion of their performance appraisal are more likely to develop actionable steps, as compared to rhetoric alone, than leaders who do not. The old adages "you can't manage what you can't don't measure" and "you treasure what you measure" ring true here as well. Our studies suggest that when leaders are accountable for diversity climate, they move beyond what they *think* about diversity to what they must *do* about diversity.

- Pay is not equivalent to personal well being. While this adage is true for all employees, our research suggests it is especially true for employees of color. Majority employees, who may find a relatively reaffirming climate across different organizations, may use pay as a primary point of differentiation. But employees of color, who instead may find wide variance in climate affirmation, may give less importance to pay in differentiating among employers. This is an especially important point for organizational leaders lacking racial awareness to consider. In general, leaders should avoid projecting their dominant values (e.g., pay) onto employees of color and instead consider that different employees may hold different value hierarchies. Organizational effectiveness will likely be improved when consideration is given to multiple value hierarchies rather than simply attending to pay and compensation, alone.

- Keep the promises you make, not just the promises you value. As our research has shown, employees of color attend, with greater intensity, to certain components of the psychological employment contract including the diversity climate promise. Leaders who only devote themselves to delivering on components of the psychological contract that are personally salient, especially if they lack racial awareness, may not deliver on components of the psychological contract that are salient to employees of color. How might this pitfall be avoided? The answer lies in being intentional in delivering on the promises made in the recruitment and selection process. If leaders will write down the superlatives they use in characterizing organizational opportunities and climate for employees of color in the selection process, and then use that checklist as a guide for delivering on the promises they made, behavior will have an increased opportunity of being shaped. The next step would be for the organization to reinforce behavior change by including and measuring diversity climate as a significant component of the employee climate survey process for department managers.

---

## INCLUSION INSIGHTS

Cumulatively, this research suggests that organizations must take four steps.

1. Move past symbolism in appointing leaders of color in favor of seeking out and developing racially aware leaders.
2. Tackle diversity climate as a systemic opportunity to improve organizational effectiveness and climate rather than a decentralized challenge for work groups.
3. Be explicit about the diversity promises made in the recruitment and selection process and manage these as proactively and intentionally as organizational processes such as safety and quality assurance.
4. Measure the extent to which the organization meets, at all levels, its promises and reinforce that behavior by including diversity climate performance in the employee survey and 360° performance review process.

Organizations that follow these four steps will leverage the value of diversity and inclusion and will, in turn, become employers of choice for top talented people, inclusive of people of color.

# 13

# Diversity and Inclusion Councils

## *Internal and External*

Trailblazers utilize every possible resource to drive inclusion and diversity into their organizations' DNA. Among the infrastructure elements required to advance this work, employee resource groups, diversity action teams or committees, and diversity councils especially are required to execute effectively on the strategy. We addressed the impact of employee resource groups and local committees and action teams in earlier chapters. In this chapter, we want to specifically explore the impact of diversity and inclusion councils. Successful inclusion and diversity efforts have an internal diversity council, or an internal plus an external diversity council. No successful initiative has existed without one or both.

## Strengthening Connectivity inside the Organization

These councils serve a powerful purpose of assisting the Trailblazers as a trusted advisor and a resource. They provide insight and information that's reflected in the organization and beyond, and they are a sounding board that managers can engage to accelerate the advancement of inclusion and diversity efforts. Councils provide a means to broadening the horizontal reach of the CEO, the CDO Trailblazer and SLT across the organization, whereas middle managers— whom we discussed in a previous chapter—provide the vertical depth of inclusion and diversity into the organization.

As Gil Casellas of Dell explains, "First and foremost was accountability. So Dell created a Global Diversity Council chaired by our CEO, Michael Dell. I have to say it's a big deal only insofar as the structure, since the CEO's commitment was always there. We just provided a design and process by which to cascade this throughout the company to get the kind of visibility and accountability it deserves." For senior leaders who report to the CEO, this work on the Global Diversity Council then becomes part of their performance objectives as a means to help drive progress deeper into the organization.

As it is with Dell, councils are typically composed of either the senior leaders who report to the CEO and/or leaders who are selected by the SLT to act on their behalf in support of the organization's inclusion and diversity efforts. These council members then liaise to the business unit and leaders who report directly to the CEO. The council leaders work closely with the CDO to ensure tight alignment with the overall inclusion and diversity and business strategies.

Diversity councils may be chaired by the CEO, jointly by the CEO and Trailblazer/CDO, or solely by the CDO. In all of these cases, the CEO visibly champions the council's work with the strong leadership support of the Trailblazer. Trailblazer companies' inclusion and diversity councils have helped them institutionalize many human capital practices that support and accelerate these initiatives. Trailblazers appreciate the value that comes with working with the Chief People Officer/HR, and they collaborate with them in regard to human capital alignment for implementation. A large part of the Trailblazers' change management work is implemented through human resources; therefore, aligning the support of the Chief People Officer/HR is critical for success in this arena.

While we've seen how important it is to have a council, it is equally vital to have the right people on it. The typical council member is a well-connected, very well respected, highly influential leader. He or she has a great deal of knowledge regarding the organization itself and the challenges and issues associated with specific business units (BUs)/functions (FXs), as well as intimate knowledge of the concerns associated with how work gets done in the organization. Trailblazers work side by side with council members to ensure they are fully aligned with the inclusion and diversity strategy as it is aligned to the overall business plan. Through the work of the councils, Trailblazers cocreate the expected outcomes and monitor strategy execution in the BUs and FXs to ensure that work is embedded into the organization at a deeper level.

Diversity councils serve as a watchdog of business relevancy and are a required resource for effective strategy implementation.

---

### INCLUSION INSIGHTS

**Responsibilities of the Inclusion and Diversity Council**

- Assist the Trailblazer/CDO in the cocreation of the inclusion and diversity strategy
- Help define and direct the organizational assessment of these initiatives' current state and ongoing milestones
- Identify barriers present in existing human resources practices that may affect recruitment, assignments and advancement, retention, education and training, mentoring, and communications
- Cocreate interventions and remedies to address issues associated with any barriers to full talent utilization
- Cocreate organizational metrics and scorecard used for tracking progress
- Conduct organizational audits and assessments to monitor and track BU and FX progress
- Feed forward and attest to the validity of the progress associated with each BU and FX diversity and inclusion plan
- Provide feedback information to their BU/FX leader and leadership team regarding comparative progress to the overall organization
- Cocreate the content and communication messages for the communication department to use

*(continued)*

(*continued*)

- Define inclusion and diversity–specific education content for the learning department to use in professional development
- Partner with the learning department to plan and implement the roll out of diversity education
- Share organizational knowledge and best practices; learn from other council members
- Become change agents and a resource to the organization as people with inclusion and diversity dilemmas and success stories seek to share
- Become internal and external spokespersons regarding progress and challenges for the work the organization is achieving with regard to inclusion and diversity

Internal diversity councils typically consist of one person who represents a business unit or major function. In general, councils range in size from six to twelve people who tend to be direct reports to the direct reports of the CEO. Said another way, the council members are ideally three levels or less from the CEO. CEO = level 1; CEO direct reports = level 2, Inclusion and Diversity Council members = level 3. See Figure 13.1.

### Selection Criteria for Inclusion and Diversity Council Members

- Influential
- Well-respected; known for acting with integrity, especially during difficult conversations
- Results-oriented
- Ethical, with strong sense of fairness
- Able to navigate successfully; knows how work gets done in the organization
- Demonstrates collaborative decision making
- Good listener; open to different ideas

- Good communicator; persuasive
- Strategic thinker
- Takes a holistic view; acts functionally or with the business unit in mind
- Minimum of three years' tenure in the company

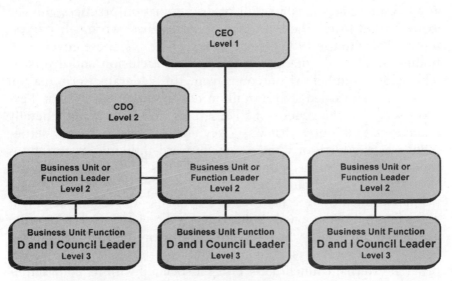

**FIGURE 13.1** Internal Inclusion Diversity Council Structure

## External Diversity Councils: Inviting the Outside In

While not a large number of organizations have utilized external diversity councils (EDCs) as a resource, those that have—voluntarily and involuntarily—declare that these groups have been instrumental in driving accountability for change. When voluntarily implemented, external diversity councils function as proactive governance bodies that are driven to help their companies accelerate diversity and inclusion efforts in key focus areas.

Over the years, and for various reasons, only a few of the Fortune 500 and 100 organizations have implemented these EDCs to act as an employee advocate, governance body, and watchdog all in one. The groups have partnered with the organizations that commissioned them to help organizations obtain high-priority, visible traction for obtaining specific results. EDCs have systematically aided the companies they serve in identifying and embedding human capital practices and processes that drive greater inclusion and diversity results—that might not have otherwise been forthcoming.

It's well-recognized and understood in the field of inclusion and diversity how such bodies got their start. As we've previously advised, most began as a result of discrimination practices and the express need to take action today to correct past wrongs from yesterday. Prior to the 1996 case of *Roberts vs. Texaco*, these governance bodies simply did not exist in the field of inclusion and diversity. The widely publicized outcome from this federal discrimination suit—which awarded a $176 million dollar settlement against Texaco—served as the genesis of EDCs. This well-known and federally mandated Task Force that was a key element of the Texaco settlement was the birth of what several forward-thinking organizations today have as voluntarily implemented EDCs.

Overall, the Trailblazers' inclusion and diversity efforts are primarily aided by internal diversity councils. This same statement regarding internal councils holds true for The Coca-Cola Company and Steve Bucherati, who—in addition to working with an internal council—has several years of successful experiences with the court-ordered external council/Task Force associated with its 2001 settlement agreement. On the heels of what so far has been the largest racial discrimination lawsuit in history (at $192 million), The Coca-Cola Company worked with its Task Force to create substantial culture shifts within their organization and embraced the underlying issue of fairness to become recognized for its inclusion and diversity efforts. The partnership with the Task Force was so successful for the company that then-Chairman and CEO Neville Isdell voluntarily extended its work an additional year beyond its completion date in order to continue the momentum with several key focus areas.

While its Task Force has long since been dismantled, The Coca-Cola Company has continued to diligently use the insights, experiences, wisdom, and knowledge to remain one of the top companies for diversity, inclusion, and fairness.

# Fast-Forward

Given that inclusion and diversity are voluntary efforts—without any real basis in legal statutes like affirmative action and discrimination—why then would a company *voluntarily* choose to establish an EDC to work on the change management efforts? Why would a company bring a group of highly respected outsiders from multiple disciplines into its fold and reveal the good, the bad, and the ugly of its change and talent management processes and results—and expect partnership and help in return? There are some who believe that the very nature of external diversity councils seem to position them in an adversarial role to the company; however, we've found no evidence that supports that contention. Instead, like The Coca-Cola Company, we believe that partnering with an EDC is an effective means to advance and sustain inclusion and diversity.

A Google search of organizations that have external diversity councils today reveals that the use of these councils has broadened very slowly. Talk with other CDOs, and you'll find that organizations such as the federal government, some universities, and only a few other major companies have implemented councils. In a news article released February 2010, major radio-ratings provider Arbitron announced that it was adding nine members to its advisory council to increase the ethnic and technological diversity of its existing group. This step is reflective of the company's desire to become more inclusive and relevant to its broad and diverse audience of urban and metropolitan customers.

EDCs—in partnership with the companies that hired them—function primarily as advisors to accomplish two major objectives:

1. Be a catalyst and make recommendations for voluntary change.
2. Push for accountability and results.

While many firms have systems and processes in place for inclusion and diversity—and, more broadly, talent management—the objectivity of a third-party reviewer cannot be underestimated. The EDC has a vested interest in making certain that the organization it works with benefits from its oversight, insight, and request for help in creating tangible results and a culture of inclusion.

The EDC functions as a mirror to the organization. It reflects the company's inner workings and provides a reality check regarding progress—or lack thereof. It "keeps it real" in terms of giving constructive feedback regarding the organization's progress. In effect, a well-functioning EDC acts as an advisory partner and barometer to make sure that the organization is not drinking too much of its own Kool-Aid. The EDC does this through the application and introduction of constructive tension and challenges to the leadership, talent management processes, and culture of the organization.

The EDC takes the company's pulse by engaging in various dialogue sessions with operations leaders, staff, and managers, conducting data analysis reviews, and holding meetings with a range of constituencies. It also interacts with employee resource groups to remain abreast of the impact—and results—of any inclusion and diversity efforts. As part of its oversight, the EDC provides ongoing recommendations to ensure that the company does not get too complacent with the incremental progress it is likely making. An effective EDC should typically push for bigger, better, faster, bolder results. That said, it should be done in the context of something called *organizational readiness*—that is, the organization's inclination and ability to embrace and sustain the change required for the long view. The EDC continually reminds its business partner that a higher degree of effort is required to achieve the truly large-scale systems change goals that the organization says it wants.

Leaders who accept the responsibility to join an EDC are committed to sustainable results for the companies with which they partner. Their backgrounds and experiences land the role for them, and their contributions solidify their position. Their job is to communicate, educate, and help the organization accelerate progress that it has declared it wants and/or needs to make.

While it is imperative to make highly credentialed people part of the EDC, those same people must show a willingness to push, challenge, learn, and engage the business of the organization on a very personal level. They must understand the culture, the people, the clients, the customers, and the environment in which the organization conducts business. Without this intimate knowledge, the EDC could default to a "tribunal" approach; they become a group to which the company simply reports findings, and that adds little or no real value beyond optics and general oversight. The most effective EDCs recognize that their true value is in acting as partners who help the business achieve specific and tangible goals. Ideally, there should be ongoing exchanges of information and data between the EDC and the company. This will allow the organization to continuously learn new things and be in a position to apply any new lessons into its existing processes in an integrated fashion. For EDCs to be most effective, a true give-and-take partnership with respect for the other's position must exist.

External diversity councils are still relatively few in number. A review of a 2005 *DiversityInc* article reported that only five of its Top 50 Companies for Diversity had external councils. In 2006, it reported that this number had risen to 15. While this may not seem like a big jump, it was particularly significant given that the number of applicant companies vying to become one of the *DiversityInc* Top 50 had risen as well.

---

### INCLUSION INSIGHTS

- External diversity councils act as a catalyst and accelerant for change
- Search for innovative thinking and expanded approaches to drive change
- Make recommendations to enhance the organization's position as an inclusive workplace
- Review data and audit progress
- Ask the tough questions
- May cocreate objectives
- Push for sustainable and specific results
- May provide a positive "voice" in the marketplace regarding the company

---

If you're thinking of starting an internal diversity council to assist your organization in accelerating results, we would encourage you to review the checklist of considerations below. While these are not all-inclusive, they represent helpful starting points derived from companies that have found success with internal councils and may make the implementation path smoother for your company.

## Checklist: Council Considerations, Requirements, Knowledge Needed

- Knowledge of organizations' strategic business plan
- Council purpose
  - alignment to business plan
  - inclusion and diversity business case
- Talent optimization
- Marketplace and client demands
- Partnerships with the communities
- Expectations of internal constituencies
  - guiding principles of operation
- Council operating procedures and infrastructure
  - council responsibilities
  - start-up considerations
- Membership
  - size
  - selection criteria
  - member responsibilities
  - confidentiality
  - business knowledge
  - self-awareness as a change agent
- Council processes
  - charter
    - purpose
    - leadership structure
    - decision making
    - terms of service
    - replacing members
    - committee infrastructure
    - roles and responsibilities of committees
  - meetings
    - objectives
    - logistics

- frequency
- attendance requirements
- amendments to the charter
- council member education
  - self-assessment
  - personal development
  - knowledge transfer
  - performance evaluation
  - reward and recognition
- Council performance
  - implementing enterprise-wide change strategies
  - leadership support
  - partnerships with key stakeholders
  - scorecard metrics and progress
  - implementation effectiveness at business unit and function level
  - tie to organizational scorecard metrics and progress
  - codevelopment of inclusion and diversity content and messages for communications plan and education program
  - presentations to BU and/or FX committees
  - interface with employees

Most of the above also applies to both internal and external councils, but one key difference exists: External council members are paid a stipend, and these stipends will vary. Both internal and external council members typically have a sunset date for their term of service.

It is possible to benchmark this information as a means to determine how best to position your particular EDC by speaking with the few companies that have them, or consultants who have implemented them.

# 14

# Employee Resource Groups or Networks

C hange is a slow progression and not one that can be expected to occur overnight. Research studies generally cite that it takes 10 years to fully implement change strategies. When it comes to diversity and inclusion, this is no less the case. Change can take years and even decades to promote and take hold throughout the culture of an organization. Business leaders have found that there are a number of processes that solidify the necessary steps for change, whether they are intended for financial gain, cultural competency, or any other business reason. Establishing goals, setting priorities, and being able to accurately and effectively monitor the success, or lack thereof, of any aspect of change is certainly an important variable over the long term. These same business leaders, from diversity leaders to CEOs, have also realized that the existence of employee resource groups (ERGs) serves a number of purposes within the organization. ERGs may also be labeled business resource groups (BRGs) or networks. Throughout this chapter we will interchangeably use the words *employee resource groups* (ERGs) and *networks*. While the name can change from one company to the next, the concept of these groups is the same: to promote the sharing of ideas and experiences with the goal of improving the organization's talent pipeline, brand eminence, and workplace culture climate.

These networks of employees also serve a multitude of purposes for the employees themselves. They give the employees a sense of camaraderie—of not being isolated or feeling alone within the organization. They also enlighten management and the leaders of the organization to the cultural issues and nuances of the customers they wish to serve. These ERGs can help a business focus its efforts on their particular constituency group or socioethnic culture and help shape and mold the direction that the company takes with regard to certain products and servicing specific customers.

For example, advertisements that are designed with a male, 40-and-over population in mind will not likely have the same impact on young, 20-something females or males. The reverse also holds true. ERGs can act as focus groups or a Think Tank to assist the organization with marketing, professional development, and real-time customer knowledge of their constituency group.

## Networks for Business Advancement

This certainly isn't to say that a business should, or does, incorporate ERGs solely for the purpose of understanding how their culturally diverse customer base thinks, acts, or determines where to spend their money. This is simply one of the functions of the groups.

For example, Michael Collins, Managing Director of Diversity Strategies for American Airlines, discusses this idea. American Airlines is said to have had one of the first ERGs for lesbian, gay, bisexual and transgender employees (LGBT). Today, American has ERGs that include an Asian-Pacific Islander group and an Indian ERG, among 15 others. Michael states "We have sixteen ERGs and so if we thought about creating new routes to new international destinations, we engage those ERGs to help us better understand what those customer needs are. What is different for them? So these groups help to develop the menus, help to develop the reading materials that are in the seat backs, they help to develop some of the training for the people who are on those flights as well as the messaging we send to those populations. We've been very successful as a result of that."

Understanding diverse groups of individuals and different cultures means that you first have to understand the groups' thought processes, how they approach the world, as well as their view of it. The idea of utilizing the unique characteristics of a company's employees is certainly not a new one, but when it is incorporated for diversity and inclusion, its benefits can be far reaching.

ERGs can have lasting and important impact on businesses of any size. These groups, or networks, can share their experiences, their ideas and opinions, and their viewpoints with upper-level management, which can then alter the direction of the company as a whole as it pertains to products, markets, and the diversity climate. While reading newspaper articles or books can be a simple, one-dimensional method to learning about other cultures or groups, it is limited. Having these resource groups available can help mold the ideas and attitudes of upper management who are attempting to work on incorporating more efficient and sustainable diversity and inclusion into the organization.

An LGBT group will have a unique perspective on how their members are viewed and treated within the company, as well as ideas on how to move forward with the diversity and inclusion initiatives, as will a Working Parents or Veterans group.

Bill Marriott, of the hospitality company Marriott, has a commitment to inclusion and diversity and, as a result of this drive and determination, he went against his Mormon church in opposing Proposition 8 in California, which banned same-sex marriages. The LGBT community represents a significant buying power and a source of talent. ERGs can partner with Trailblazers and inform and educate other leaders in their understanding of the major issues that affect their constituency group members on an intellectual and visceral level. While a social, personal, or even a business issue may not affect one person in a direct way, it could have a dramatic impact on a group of others. By having these networks within an organization, a greater sense of understanding can be instilled throughout the organization as a whole, and that can translate into a cultural shift—an ideological revolution within that organization that can help foster a more inclusive culture for all.

## ERGs

There are a number of ERGs that mat develop at the grassroots level, or that businesses may establish for their employees. A number of cultural and ethnic groups exist within just about every company in America and many international organizations as well. If you were to walk into the corporate headquarters of some of the largest organizations, odds are you will find a representative of nearly every major constituency group.

It isn't necessary or practical to have a resource group for every group, unless there is a definitive business need for it that has been established. For example, if a company has one employee who is Native American, then having a Native American ERG would not be practical. This doesn't mean that it is irrelevant, however. There is a distinct difference between being practical and being relevant.

It is possible, though, to incorporate this individual into another type of resource group that will be able to capture this individual's experiences, ideas, and desires for the business as a whole. Some organizations have addressed this issue through Multicultural ERGs.

## Types of Employee Resource Groups

If a company sets out to establish ERGs as part of their diversity and inclusion initiative, or approves existing grassroots ERGs it is often helpful to benchmark best practices. Below is a list of some of the more commonly established ERGs though the constituency group names may vary. These represent ERGs that are currently in place by the collective Trailblazers highlighted in this book. They are:

- Native American
- African American/Black
- Asian/Pacific Islander
- Latino/Hispanic
- LGBT
- Women
- Interfaith/Faith based
- 50 and over
- GenNext (Under 35/Gen X & Y)
- Men
- Veterans

- disAbility ERG for persons with disabilities
- Parenting

Again, this is not an all-inclusive list, nor is there a limit to the types of groups that may form for business purposes within an organization. Simply reviewing this list should open up conversations regarding your ERGs and how each group can contribute to the inclusion and diversity strategy as it relates to the business objectives of the company.

If we take a look at the LGBT ERG, for instance it would not take long to realize the types of challenges this group may face. Currently, the debate rages throughout the United States about whether gays should be allowed to legally marry. While this is a social issue, it certainly impacts the workplace, whether on a conscious or subconscious level. It's nearly impossible for people to escape a topic that embroils itself on every news network and in every editorial from one week to the next.

This level of coverage in the public view inflames prejudices and hardens opinions. There may be antiquated policies within the organization or something tied to the company's mission statement that affects LGBT employees in a negative (or positive) way. By having an LGBT ERG within your organization, management may be able to get a better understanding about what employees face on a regular basis and how this group can use their resources to help the business grow.

Setting up the opportunity for ERGs to share their opinions, experiences, and ideas that impact them and the business offers them empowerment and help shape the culture of the company.

Considerations and first step in starting or supporting an ERG:

- Determine the need.
  - Not every employee within the organization will have a need for a resource group.
  - Align to the diversity and inclusion strategy and how would an ERG will affect this goal.
- Determine the executive liason.
  - This is the avenue by which the ideas discussed will be brought to management's attention.
- Determine group membership requirements.

- Communicate that ERGs will be open to all employees; irrespective of whether they are a member of the particular constituency group.
- Determine who wants to commit to the group and effect positive change/forward momentum?
- Define the parameters and logistics for the operations of the group.
- Define how often the group will meet.
  - Once a month?
  - Once every other month?
  - More frequently?
  - Less frequently?

## Chaired by Senior Management

Seventy-one percent of the companies we interviewed have senior leader who chairs their ERGs, and who, in turn, report directly to the CEO. This creates a direct link between the discussions that go on in the meetings and the top-level management. Is it important or critical that this link be established? Trailblazer companies believe this link is critical in order to ensure that ERGs are part of the overall inclusion and diversity strategy that supports the business. Otherwise there is a risk that ERGs may be perceived as separate, and perhaps seen as social groups not related to furthering the inclusion and diversity business strategy. It is true that some organizations have not made the link between ERGs and senior management, but the experiences of the Trailblazers is best practice.

Think about a time when you may have been part of a group discussion, where the topic incited passion, and the ideas were flowing freely. Perhaps a college organization or group might fall into this category. When emotions are stirred, opinions can be varied and impassioned. If the group is left to monitor itself, while the ideas will (hopefully) reach the senior management, the importance of the ideas discussed could be lost in interpretation.

Reports, e-mails, memos, and such are dry and devoid of emotion. There are certainly a number of different methods that can go into the presentation to help create or categorize the depth of the ideas as well as their importance, but without direct observation, the same intensity will often fade and be lost.

If a company is making a concerted and meaningful effort to develop ERGs, then it is critical to have senior management chair these groups.

## A Deeper Look at ERGs/Networks and D & I

As Deb Dagit explains about Merck's diversity and inclusion initiative, "I would say that what we've done through the D & I strategy, throughout global constituency group as well as our ERGs, is to provide a communications channel where both our employees and our employees' social networks on a global basis can inform our thinking about the needs of different populations on a global basis so that we are providing critical intelligence to different parts of our business."

These networks are designed to be formal, not informal, avenues through which employees can share their ideas. "We have formal avenues. One we formed about eighteen months ago, global constituency groups that collectively represent our global workforce. There are men and women, which are both inclusive of multicultural men and women. We have Black, Hispanic, Latino, Native and Indigenous peoples, Asia Pacific; we also have interfaith, which we define as all denominations as well as agnostics. We also have a generational team which we define as thirty and under and fifty and over in the same group. We have a differently abled and an LGBT group and collectively people find themselves in one of those ten teams on a global basis. These teams are made up of senior leaders that are representative of all our different business units and geographies. And the cochairs, except for the men and women groups, are male and female and one is inside the U.S. and one outside the U.S."

"The executive sponsors are leaders at the top of the organizations who are not a member of that group so they can learn about a group that is different from their own but also engage in unfettered advocacy as a sponsor."

When asked whether these executive chairs are on the executive committee, Deb Dagit explained, "The CEO and I looked to find appropriate executive sponsors for a couple of the teams. We went outside that group. So, for instance, the head of our vaccines division who doesn't report directly to the CEO has our interfaith executive sponsorship, which is a great match because in our vaccine's portfolio we have Gardasil, which is a product that protects against sexually transmitted disease, HPV. There were a lot of issues of faith in getting that product into the market in a manner that is respectful of faiths that teach abstinence.

"So we also try to make a match from a business standpoint with what made the most sense. Then also another individual, the one that is the executive sponsor for our generational team is someone who is playing a really critical role in our global sales and marketing efforts. He is someone who had experience at another pharmaceutical company in leveraging the workforce to inform the diversity efforts. And he is playing a critical role in our merger. So he was someone who, although not again a direct report to the CEO, had a lot of passion and energy around this work, a lot of practical experience around leveraging employee information to inform strategies.

"In the marketplace in the sales and marketing arena we know that for people under thirty and people over fifty, there are some interesting marketplace trends around how people prefer to get information for different reasons.

"The other thing I would say from an internal workforce standpoint, these populations have a lot to offer each other as well in terms of knowledge transfer, reciprocal learning, and mentoring and finding ways to collaborate so that the frustrations that younger workers feel about career path development and the frustrations that people over fifty feel about being stereotyped as being not as technologically savvy can be overcome, for example. There is a lot they can offer each other because of the unfortunate tendency to over generalize about generations at work.

"But, by being each other's advocates, they can mitigate some of that."

## Rewards and Recognition

The work that can go into an ERG can be significant, especially for the employees who are a part of that group. While these groups are voluntary and a great way to boost one's position within the company, other rewards and recognitions could be considered because of their lasting impact on the employees, as well as their peers.

Michael Collins, of American Airlines, talks about the recognition program they have in place: "At the end of the year we recognize their accomplishments formally at a luncheon. One of the other ways we recognize them is each ERG has an executive sponsor and that is someone who is a Vice President or higher as well as a number of manager sponsors in the organization."

"They participate and provide support and direction for the ERG. They also send a message to the organization that this is important. So between that and also participating in the events they have throughout the year, I think those are some big ways they are recognized."

Improving a company's diversity and inclusion efforts can certainly be one way for employees to be motivated to participate in ERGs and networks, but offering recognition beyond the normal realm of the business can be a way to motivate others to want to become involved. When others are motivated, then the process continues to build, bringing the company closer to its ultimate goal of diversity and inclusion.

# A Question of Faith

One challenge, or at least one thing that may appear to be a challenge on the surface, is having conflicted viewpoints within two or more different and unique resource groups. For example, at American Airlines, there is a Christian ERG as well as an LGBT ERG.

Taking into account the current political climate mentioned previously, the social debate that has pitted religious groups against gay and lesbian rights activists would seem to pose a major dilemma for these different ERGs within the company. After all, if one group has an opinion or idea that contradicts the other group's ideas, then couldn't this lead to animosity, distrust, or resentment?

According to Michael Collins, "We have one guiding principle for all ERGs and that is they have to be collaborative in nature and have to provide value to the business and be focused on the business. So it's okay to be different as long as it's not at the expense of someone else. That has worked very well.

"American Airlines is here in Dallas/Ft. Worth and I think it's safe to say it's the Bible Belt. There is also a pretty good concentration of gay and lesbian people here in the Dallas area as well. So we started from a place of inclusion and collaboration. And everyone understands. I think that has helped us to achieve a healthy balance over the years. Yes, both of those ERGs are still in existence. They are probably the largest two ERGs with the African American ERG being a very close third."

## Tracking Employee Resource Groups

When developing ERGs, it's a good idea to monitor and require information regarding the effectiveness of the ERGs on an annual basis. This is especially true when the organization conducts business in various geographies and countries and is made easier through a scorecard. The larger the company, the more important it is to have tracking in place.

In any organization, the goal is to effect change—in this case diversity and inclusion; tracking the progress as well as the results are important. This goes for any ERG that is established for D & I. As Michael Collins adds, "We do track membership. There are about 4,000 people around the system that are engaged in some form of ERG. We also have a Diversity Advisory Council, which consists of two people from each ERG, and they get together once every month and talk about what they're doing, why they're doing it, to share their experiences, and also leverage their strengths."

As we have already discussed in Chapter 13, the advisory councils and boards can be an integral part of the success of any diversity and inclusion effort within an organization.

## More Than One Way to Achieve Results

It should become obvious that there is no right or wrong method of achieving diversity and inclusion within an organization. While the efforts set forth for ERGs will begin the process, it takes the concerted effort of dedicated employees and management to sustain progress and succeed.

This success can be brought about with or without ERGs, and without advisory boards, but for the Trailblazers, the use of one or more of these methods helps accelerate the practices associated with achieving results with inclusion and diversity. ERGs offer the company's employees the chance to become more empowered, to help mold and shape the course of the company into the future, not just for cultural diversity and benefit, but also to focus marketing and research designs toward different groups.

Looking back at the list of different groups (which, remember, is not all-inclusive), they can cover nearly all cultural, ethnic, gender, religious, and other groups. The principle comes down to choosing which groups will benefit your company's employees and business the most.

## Budgets for ERGs

It's important to note that 100 percent of the Trailblazers companies have a budget for their ERGs. What this money is used for within the groups will certainly be determined by the company, and possibly the groups themselves, but leaving an ERG without the means necessary to move forward and accomplish their goals could be tantamount to trying to advertise a new product or service without any kind of budget.

More than half of the Trailblazers interviewed stated that their aggregate annual budget for ERGs was greater than $16,000, but might be as little as a few thousand dollars. Each company has its own goals and priorities, and it's important to remember that ERGs must have some funding in order to achieve the best results.

## A Word about Social Networking

The age of Facebook, Twitter, and other social networking sites has created massive potential for businesses to expand their diversity and inclusion initiatives. We suggest you consider a limited use of social networking platforms to allow your employees to connect with one another, as well as others outside of the organization, to help learn more about different cultures and expectations. In doing so, your company will  forge greater connectivity to your employees and to the community and become better known as a diverse and global enterprise.

Success is measured in steps. ERGs and networks are important steps in the long journey toward inclusion and diversity.

# 15

# Supplier Diversity

## A *Strategic Procurement Choice*

---

Diversity and inclusion doesn't end in the workplace. It extends and expands into regions and communities and geographies that stretch far beyond an organization's human capital. How a business manages their influence and external footprint can have a great and lasting impact throughout many other businesses and organizations. A business has a responsibility not only to its customers, but also its community, shareholders, and employees. One enlightened way organizations demonstrate direct influence and impact is through their choice of suppliers. Although supplier diversity has been a more recent component of the diversity and inclusion strategy for many organizations (last 10 years), it is fast becoming a major focus within the United States and globally. Trailblazers see supplier diversity as a win-win-win for all stakeholders. Less forward-thinking businesses only see it as a compliance-based action when conducting business with the government.

As the current economy is now more widely recognized to be a global one, companies no longer look at supplier diversity as a hindrance to their global aspirations and goals. These companies are

**205**

discovering that supplier diversity efforts resonate on a U.S. level, even as they operate their business on a global platform. Some businesses connect their supplier diversity with their sustainability efforts, which is a real plus as organizations look for ways to support communities, reduce their carbon footprint, and be more responsible community citizens.

Businesses are pressured to find ways to save money, cut spending, and consolidate their supply base. The idea of supplier diversity, then, can seem to be an antithesis to this effort due to the outreach and education efforts sometimes needed to enable minority- and women-owned business enterprise (MWBE) as well as small, disadvantaged companies to compete. But Trailblazers are defying expectations by proving that the effect of these efforts are profitable.

When communities observe and experience the efforts of a corporation to support MWBEs there are both tangible and intangible results. These communities, then, are more apt to support the corporations, thereby increasing sales and thus increasing demand for the suppliers.

Trailblazers are committed to supplier diversity. It makes good business sense. Eight of the 12 companies featured employ full-time staff dedicated exclusively to managing and growing supplier diversity. Ninety percent offer training and education to women- and minority-owned businesses interested in learning the procedures of working with their companies. Trailblazers and other progressive companies see MWBEs as their partners and treat them as such for the good of all.

## First Tier, Second Tier—Where to Focus?

When discussing supplier diversity, one of the topics that often comes up is the level of spending. The larger the business, or the corporation, the fewer the suppliers they typically wish to deal with. The entire process is a chain and each tier of supplier is a link in the chain. A large corporation often will interact with large first tier or prime suppliers which, in turn, will subcontract with smaller second tier vendors.

For example, when a homeowner orders electric service from a utility company, they typically don't deal with anyone except their first tier supplier—the company to whom they write their monthly checks. Yet, in many cases throughout the country, these large electric companies are also buying their power from a variety of smaller sources, i.e. second tier suppliers.

In corporations, the same concept holds true. While these large businesses will deal almost entirely with the first tier suppliers, there may be limits to the number of capable MWBE, just based on sheer capacity and size as well as limits to the number of MWBEs an organization directly uses before it loses efficiencies of scale and cost. However, according to the U.S. Census, minority-owned businesses have exceeded non-minority-owned businesses in growth for more than a decade, thus making the issue of scarcity a diminishing challenge. Corporations have found that their influence is not strictly one-dimensional. In others words, much like the homeowner who can now determine what percentage of their electricity is generated by renewable energy, businesses can place pressure on their tier one suppliers to utilize diverse suppliers on the second and third tier levels. We have found this to be true with some of our clients whereby they are told by their business customers to report to them the number of minority suppliers used and the gross expenditures for the projects completed with MWBEs. Trailblazer Elizabeth Campbell, Partner and Chief Diversity Officer at Andrews Kurth LLP proactively supplies corporate clients with the firm's diversity actions and results even if they have not asked for the information. The tracking of hours related to D & I (a process she created for the firm) helps clients appreciate the importance the firm places on diversity.

Just because a business is limited on the number of potential suppliers with whom they deal directly, it doesn't mean that they can't effect change and inclusion on other levels. Some small companies may have few or nonexistent first tier suppliers, but, as with GM, for example, they demand that their first tier suppliers purchase at least 8 percent of their supplies from certified minority and women suppliers.

By partnering as a second tier supplier, many MWBEs have the opportunity to engage in commerce with larger corporations and are able to compete in a market that may have seemed out of reach in the past.

## Supplier Diversity at Its Core

So what exactly are certified minority and women suppliers? The National Minority Supplier Development Council (NMSDC) and the Women's Business Enterprise National Council (WBENC) have very strict requirements on what constitutes a minority- or woman-owned business. The NMSDC and WBENC have a database of thousands of MWBE businesses in the United States, encompassing a wide range of businesses. When an organization seeks to incorporate supplier diversity into their business model, they can turn to WBEMC or NMSDC for a list of certified women and minority suppliers.

In order to be certified as an MWBE, the supplier must meet specific requirements. These requirements are:

- The supplier business must be 51 percent owned and controlled by a member of a specific racial group or be a woman.
- They must be registered with the state.
- They must have solid company management and financial viability.
- The owners of the business must be U.S. citizens.

In order to be considered a minority, the individual must be able to prove through documentation that they belong to one of the following ethnic groups, and in the case of WBENC, be a woman:

- Asian-Indian
- Asian-Pacific
- Black
- Hispanic
- Native American

MWBEs employ members of their immediate community and have a direct financial impact on the region in which they operate through the money they spend and bring in. When a business, whether through first or second tier spending, collaborates with MWBEs, their impact is felt throughout the community in a ripple effect.

It should be noted that we recommend women- and minority-owned business owners complete the various certifications in order to increase their odds of securing contracts from corporations.

# Does Supplier Diversity Translate into Results for the Business?

Supplier diversity can benefit a business. It is the act of conscience that helps to boost the morale of the business's employees, management, and its customers as well. Second, when the community begins to realize the conscious decision, influence, and impact the larger business has on supplier diversity, these consumers focus their purchasing power more directly on the larger business. Third, when businesses expand their supplier diversity efforts to include the diverse groups they recognize internally, such as veterans, people with disAbilities, and the LGBT community, people both internally and externally recognize the corporation as being congruent in their commitment to D & I.

Trailblazers track dollars spent with MWBEs. It has been found that even if a diverse supplier is only operating on a local level, that boost from the larger business often allows the diverse supplier to expand and grow to a regional, national, or even global level. Once the cycle starts, these MWBEs become and integral part of the procurement process.

## *Opportunity* Is the Key Word

Opportunity is perhaps the most important word to consider when dealing with supplier diversity. While the corporation itself benefits, such as unique products, often greater agility with regard to production design, it is the *opportunity* presented to the MWBEs that matters most. MWBEs/entrepreneurs represent the greatest growth area in today's economy.

A corporation's responsibility, then, is to help these diverse suppliers develop, grow, and be competitive in or to work with or compete with the larger suppliers.

If every member of a company's management team were asked to consider the opportunities that they were afforded throughout their professional lives, and determined how those opportunities affected where they are today, nearly all would admit to having had some form of outside influence, whether in the form of a mentor or friend or colleague who pointed them in the right direction or put them in contact with someone that helped improve their position. Engaging in supplier diversity is part of the engine that fuels our economy's growth. Trailblazer companies simply see this as good business, one that makes good business sense.

## Reaching Out to Diverse Suppliers

Seeking out supplier diversity can be daunting in the earliest stages. Where to find these diverse suppliers can pose a number of challenges for many business leaders. There are a number of ways to go about seeking quality diverse suppliers for first or second tier.

A good starting point can be any, or all, of the following:

- Utilize company diversity councils and employee resource groups (ERGs) to surface names of diverse suppliers (see Chapter 13 and 14) for more information on boards and councils and ERGs).
- Join the National Minority Supplier Development Council (NMSDC).
- Contact the Women's Business Enterprise National Council (WBENC).
- Network with diverse suppliers through trade shows.
- Meet diverse suppliers through business forums that are often hosted by community diversity councils and Chambers of Commerce.
- Identify and then attend the meetings of targeted Chambers of Commerce such as the Asian Chamber of Commerce; the Women's Chamber of Commerce; the Black Chamber of Commerce; the Hispanic Chamber of Commerce, and others.

When seeking to incorporate supplier diversity, it's important to be as transparent as possible. When a company remains open and transparent about its goals with its suppliers, and actively pursues supplier diversity, it will continue to impact the suppliers on down the list of tiers. When suppliers understand that diversity is a priority for a company, they tend to respond accordingly.

# Defining Goals within a Company

## Pitney Bowes

Defining the goals within a company has always been important in being able to achieve those stated goals. As Susan Johnson, Vice President Strategic Management and Diversity Leadership for Pitney Bowes, states eloquently: "Way back to the early 1990s when we put together a diversity task force they had two directives. One [was that] they needed to define what diversity meant at Pitney Bowes and then they had to put in place a process whereby we would measure it."

There are a number of ways to go about defining and measuring goals when it comes to supplier diversity, so it is important to determine which method will work best for the company as a whole, and the leadership core as a group. There is nothing more detrimental to a cause than an inability to state clearly defined goals and method of measurement.

Susan went on to explain, "For many, many years we used both a quantitative and qualitative measure, a set of metrics that were categorized into five different areas, pretty typical areas. Workplace representation, of course, but also staffing and development, community involvement, and supplier diversity.

"Each one of our lines of business would say what they were going to do in those five areas and then define what good, better, and best performance would look like. Then we would hold them accountable for it and align the results against it with their incentive compensation."

As can be clearly seen through Susan Johnson's account, the entire process of diversity—and more importantly to this chapter, supplier diversity—is that the process takes time to develop. Without the proper metrics in place, and without a strong and clearly defined goal that is transparent to not only the business itself, but also to the first tier suppliers with which the company deals, then the road to success becomes much steeper and more heavily shrouded in the fog of missed opportunities.

## Andrews Kurth, LLP

As Elizabeth Campbell, Partner and Chief Diversity Officer at Andrews Kurth, LLP, discusses supplier diversity and procurement, "What we've done is look at what I'll call 'attorney engagement'" around diversity and inclusion. Are we making sure people are getting involved in our diversity and inclusion activities?" To track engagement Elizabeth launched a process similar to "billable hours," which attorneys were already accustomed to recording.

When client companies asked about the firm's diversity efforts, including supplier diversity, she was able to deliver tangible evidence supporting all D & I efforts. She shared that "by the end of my first year, by the end of 2007, we had rolled out a billing system for all the timekeepers, all the lawyers in the firm. We have roughly four hundred lawyers. So we're running somewhere in the neighborhood of 3,000 hours a year in diversity from zero. That is meaningful to me because that begins to measure attorney engagement. Not only are they participating but they are taking the time to write it down, and I'm tracking it and I can see what is going on."

As can be seen through Elizabeth's example, measuring the associated time spent on D & I efforts and keeping open communications with all parties involved has an important impact on the success of diversity and inclusion as a whole. When talking about supplier diversity, this open communication should extend to the first tier suppliers as well to set their expectations regarding collaboration.

These efforts will then transfer down the line to the second and third tier suppliers, and eventually to the customers.

## Measures of Success

Supplier diversity is an important factor for businesses to incorporate into their D & I strategy.

---

### INCLUSION INSIGHTS

- Establish full-time supplier diversity postion within the strategic procurement function.
- Start with a specific goal. Define the measurement of success.
  - Do you want to increase supplier diversity by 5 percent this year? How about 10 percent? Can you achieve this through first tier? Are first tier MWBEs available?

- Set a specific strategy to achieve the goal.
  - Will you change a supplier to accomplish this goal?
  - What influence can you impress on first tier suppliers to purchase from MWBE's second and third tier suppliers?
- Track spending through suppliers and your systems.
- Survey your current suppliers.
- Report results.

# Appendix
# Study Methodology and Samples

## Study I: Survey of Business School Deans

In our first project, we contacted leaders of all 658 U.S. AACSB business schools (Association to Advance Collegiate Schools of Business) to invite their participation in the study of diversity policies and practices. One hundred forty-three leaders participated in the research, for a response rate of 22 percent. Comparison of the respondent sample with the population of AACSB school leaders indicated the sample was representative of the population. Demographic data for the sample are summarized below. We used a combination of Web and postal surveys for data collection. In our data analysis, we employed statistical techniques including correlation, factor analysis, estimates of reliability (Cronbach's alpha), and regression controlling for possible effects of demographic variables including sex, age, ethnicity, time in position, and school type. We developed our own measure of extent of diversity activities (the scale was published in 2006; items are shown in Table A.1 in the body of the Appendix) and used scales developed by other diversity scholars to measure aspects of the diversity climate. The findings of this research are presented in our 2006 article in the *Journal of Managerial Issues*, the 2007 article in *Journal of Business Ethics*, and the 2009 article in *International Journal of Human Resource Management*. The results from this first project, which we report in this Appendix, were statistically significant.

# Study 1 Demographic Data

Demographic characteristics of our business school leader participants are summarized in Table A.1.

**Table A.1** Study 1 Demographic Data

|  | Number | Percent |
|---|---|---|
| **Sex** | | |
| Male | 90 | 73 |
| Female | 33 | 27 |
| **Ethnicity** | | |
| White | 103 | 82 |
| Hispanic | 3 | 2 |
| African American | 11 | 9 |
| U.S. born Asian | 2 | 2 |
| Native American | 2 | 2 |
| Non U.S. born | 5 | 4 |
| **Current Position** | | |
| Dean | 92 | 72 |
| Asst./Assoc. Dean | 28 | 22 |
| Other | 7 | 6 |
| **Age** | | |
| Mean | 54.4 years | |
| Standard deviation | 6.5 | |
| **Years in Current Position** | | |
| Mean | 4.7 years | |
| Standard deviation | 5.4 | |
| **University Type** | | |
| Four year private college | 26 | 20 |
| Four year public college | 21 | 16 |
| Private doctoral degree granting university | 6 | 5 |
| Private non-doc. degree granting university | 8 | 6 |
| Public university doc. degree granting university | 46 | 36 |
| Public university non-doc. degree granting university | 22 | 17 |

# Study 2: Survey of Business School Faculty of Color

In our second project, we contacted all 658 members of the PhD Project networking alumnae group to invite their participation in the study of the effect of (business school) diversity climate on professional employee of color outcomes, including organizational commitment and turnover intentions. Of the faculty of color in the database with valid e-mail addresses, 182 (27.5%) completed the survey. Demographic data for the sample are summarized below. We used an online survey to collect the data. We used established, published scales to measure dimensions of the diversity climate and employee of color outcomes (organizational commitment and turnover intentions). For more information about the scales we used, please see the articles reporting the details of our studies. In our data analysis, we employed statistical techniques including correlation, principal components factor analysis with varimax rotation, estimates of reliability (Cronbach's alpha), and hierarchical regression controlling for possible effects of demographic variables including sex, age, ethnicity, time in position, and school type. We controlled for multicollinearity using Aiken and West's (1991) procedure.[1] We followed Baron and Kenny's (1986) three-condition analytical procedure to test for mediation.[2] Results of the second project to date are published in our 2010 article in the *Journal of Business Ethics*. In addition, we have an article in press at *Career Development International*. The results from the second project that we report in this chapter were statistically significant.

# Study 2 Demographic Data

Demographic characteristics of our professional faculty of color study participants are summarized in Table A.2.

**Table A.2** Study 2 Demographic Data

|  | Number | Percent |
|---|---|---|
| *Sex* | | |
| Male | 113 | 62 |
| Female | 69 | 38 |
| *Ethnicity* | | |
| White | 9 | 5 |
| Hispanic | 39 | 21 |
| African American | 116 | 64 |
| U.S. born Asian | 7 | 4 |
| Native American | 9 | 5 |
| "Other" | 2 | 1 |
| *Current Position* | | |
| Professor | 173 | 95 |
| Instructor | 4 | 2 |
| Administrator or Other | 6 | 3 |
| *Age* | | |
| Mean | 45.5 years | |
| Standard deviation | 9.4 | |
| *Years in Current Position* | | |
| Mean | 6.9 years | |
| Standard deviation | 6.5 | |
| *University Type* | | |
| Four year college | 84 | 46 |
| Non-doctoral degree granting institution | 24 | 13 |
| Doctoral degree granting institution | 74 | 41 |

# Notes

## CHAPTER 2

1. Kotter, John P. (1996). *Leading Change*, p. 48. Boston, Massachusetts: Harvard Business School Press.

## CHAPTER 3

1. Lombardo, Michael M., & Eichinger, Robert W. (2006). *FYI For Your Improvement*[TM] *4th Edition. A Guide for Development and Coaching for Learners, Managers, Mentors and Feedback Givers.* Lominger International.

## CHAPTER 7

1. Kalev, A., "Best Practices or Best Guesses," *American Sociological Review*, August 2006, pp. 589–617, University of Arizona.
2. Ibid, p. 611.
3. *DiversityInc. Magazine*. January 2006.

## CHAPTER 8

1. *USA Today*, March 8. 2010.
2. Gallagher Hateley, B.J., & Schmidt, Warren H. *A Peacock in the Land of Penguins*, 2001. The video of this fable can be found on several web sites.
3. "Global Diversity and Inclusion: Perceptions, Practices and Attitudes." A Study for the Society of Human Resource Management (SHRM) conducted by the Economist Unit. Findings released 2010.
4. "Donald" is a fictitious name used to protect the identity of the real person.
5. *Fortune Magazine*, "Why Mentoring Works."
6. www.Catalyst.org.

## CHAPTER 12

1. Beaton, A., & Tougas, F. (2001). Reactions to Affirmative Action: Group membership and social justice. *Social Justice Research*, 141, 61–78. Konrad, A. & Linnehan, F. (1995). Race and sex differences in line managers' reactions to equal employment opportunity and AA interventions. *Group and Organization Management*, 20, 409–439. Parker, C., Baltes, B., & Christiansen, N. (1997). Support for affirmative action, justice perceptions, and work attitudes: A study of gender and racial-ethnic group differences. *Journal of Applied Psychology*, 82, 376–389.

2. *Ibid.*

3. Helms, J. (1990). *Black and white racial identity. Theory, research and practice.* *New York*: Greenwood Press.

4. Neville, H., Lilly, R., Duran, G., Lee, R., & Browne, L. (2000). Construction and initial validation of the Color-Blind Racial Attitudes Scale (CoBRAS). *Journal of Counseling Psychology*, 47, 59–70.

5. Linnehan, F., Chrobot-Mason, D., & Konrad, A. (2002). The importance of ethnic identity to attitudes, norms, and behavioral intentions toward diversity. Paper presented at the Academy of Management meeting, Denver.

6. Ross, L. (1977). The intuitive psychologist and his shortcomings. In L. Berkowitz (Ed.), *Advances in experimental social psychology*. Orlando, FL: Academic Press.

7. Buttner, E. H., Lowe, K. B., & Billings-Harris, L. (2007). Impact of leader racial attitude on ratings of causes and solutions for an employee of color shortage. *Journal of Business Ethics*, 73, 129–144.

8. Shinn, S. (2003). Minority report. *BizEd*, a publication of the Association to Advance Collegiate Schools of Business (AACSB), St Louis, MO, March/April, 30–35.

9. Van Knippenberg, D., De Dreu, C. K. W., & Homan, A. C. (2004). Work group diversity and group performance: An integrative model and research agenda. *Journal of Applied Psychology*, 89(6), 1008–1022.

10. Turner, C., & Myers, S., Jr. (2000). *Faculty of Color in Academe: Bittersweet Success*. Boston: Allyn & Bacon.

11. Kossek, E. E., & Zonia, S. C. (1993). Assessing diversity climate: A field study of reactions to employer efforts to promote diversity. *Journal of Organizational Behavior*, 14, 61–81.

12. Mor Barak, M. E., Cherin, D. & Berkman, S. (1998). Organizational and personal dimensions in diversity climate. *Journal of Applied Behavioral Science*, 34, 82–104.

13. Roberson, Q. M., & Stevens, C. K. (2006). Making Sense of Diversity in the Workplace: Organizational Justice and Language Abstraction in

Employees? Accounts of Diversity-related Incidents. *Journal of Applied Psychology*, 91: 379.

14. Hopkins, W., Hopkins S., and Mallette, P. (2001). Diversity and Managerial Value Commitment: A Test of Some Proposed Relationships. *Journal of Managerial Issues* 13 (3): 288–306.

15. Carr, J. Z., Schmidt, A. M., Ford, J. K., & DeShon, R. P. (2003). Climate perceptions matter: A meta-analytic path analysis relating molar climate, cognitive and affective states, and individual level work outcomes. *Journal of Applied Psychology*, 88, 587–619.

16. Simons, T., Friedman, R., Liu, L. A. & McLean Parks, J. (2007). Racial differences in sensitivity to behavioral integrity: Attitudinal consequences, in-group effects and 'trickle down' among black and non-black employees. *Journal of Applied Psychology*, 92(3), 650–665.

17. Hicks-Clarke, D., & Iles, P. (2000). Climate for diversity and its effects on career and organisational attitudes and perceptions. *Personnel Review*, Vol. 29 Iss: 3, pp. 324–345.

18. Schulte, M., Ostroff, C., & Kinicki, A. (2006). Organizational climate systems and psychological climate perceptions: A cross-level study of climate-satisfaction relationships. *Journal of Occupational and Organizational Psychology*, 79, 645–671.

19. Chrobot-Mason, D. (2003). Keeping the promise: Psychological contract violations for minority employees. *Journal of Managerial Psychology*, 18, 22–45.

20. Buttner, E. H., Lowe, K. B., & Billings-Harris, L. (2010). The impact of diversity promise fulfillment on professionals of color outcomes in the U.S. *Journal of Business Ethics*, 91, 501–518.

21. Rousseau, D. M. (1989). Psychological and implied contracts in organizations. *Employee Responsibilities and Rights Journal*, 2, 131–139.

22. Bies, R., & Moag, J. S. (1986). Interactional justice: Communication criteria for fairness. in B. Sheppard (Ed.), *Research on negotiation in organizations, Vol. 1.* Greenwich, CT: JAI Press, 43–55.

23. McKay, P., Avery, D., Tonidandel, S., Morris, M., Hernandez, M., & Hebl, M. R. (2007). Racial differences in employee retention: Are diversity climate perceptions the key? *Personnel Psychology*, 60, 35–62.

24. McKay, P., Avery, D., & Morris, M. (2008). Mean racial-ethnic differences in employee sales performance: The moderating role of diversity climate. *Personnel Psychology*, 61, 349–374.

25. Shinn, S. (2003). Minority report. *BizEd*, a publication of the Association to Advance Collegiate Schools of Business (AACSB), St Louis, MO, March/April, 30–35.

## APPENDIX

1. Aiken, L. S., & West, S. G. (1991). Multiple Regression: Testing and interpreting interactions. Newbury Park, CA: Sage.

2. Baron, R. M., & Kenny, D. A. (1986). The Moderator-Mediator variable distinction in Social Psychological research: Conceptual, strategic, and statistical considerations. *Journal of Personality and Social Psychology*, 51, 1173–1182.

# Index